FOREWORD
BY
OLIN W. STRATTON

This book has been published in order to fill a long unmet need for more information about the heritage of the state of Illinois. Because of the perfect mix of classic Misselhorn art, meticulous historical research, interesting and unusual information (and functional indexing), teachers will find this book a valuable asset and time saver.

History buffs and families who want to pursue learning experiences, in combination with short trips, will find this book an excellent guide for enrichment and knowledge. Libraries, from middle school through university levels, will want to add this book to their shelves. It should also find a place in the home libraries of all nostalgia buffs.

Roscoe Misselhorn has, for the most part, become well known for his pencil sketches of barns, covered bridges, steamboats, trains, historical buildings, and masterpieces of nature. Because of his realistic approach, he is often known as the Norman Rockwell of the midwest. The drawings in this book were done over a long period of time ranging from the 1920's to some which were done in 1985.

A very prolific artist, Misselhorn has successfully tried his hand at all kinds of art ranging from his pencil drawings to commercial art, political cartoons, and full scale murals. The first wood cut he ever did was selected by the Library of Congress to be part of an art show that was sent to museums all over the country (The Carnegie Institute was probably the most famous of all the places it was shown). Although Roscoe Misselhorn is currently listed as a graduate of Washington University School of Art (which he attended in the twenties) his talent was clearly evident by the time he was in the third grade. Now in his eighties, Misselhorn's incredible talent and speed have produced many masterpieces. It has been a pleasure to know and to work with Roscoe Misselhorn and his wife Ruth.

Dedicated to Ruth Misselhorn
whose loyal devotion for over 61 years has
made it possible for countless thousands of people
to enjoy Misselhorn art

Illinois
SKETCHES
by
Roscoe Misselhorn

edited by Elaine Stratton

Research Director—Cerridgwyn Pyrs

published by

SWISS VILLAGE BOOK STORE
Highland & Laclede's Landing

Jeffrey Stratton—Marketing Director

CONTENTS

NATURAL BRIDGE—Shawnee National Forest—Pomona

There are a number of natural bridges in Southern Illinois—all are arches spanning valleys. This one is the best known of the seven. It is also probably one of the most spectacularly beautiful, although nearby Giant City State Park is renowned for its gigantic and unusual rock formations.

Pomona Natural Bridge spans about ninety feet from end to end and, at its thinnest section near the middle, it is only about six feet wide. There is about a twenty-five foot drop to the valley floor below the arch. The little stream that spent a few million years washing away rock to produce such a pleasing sight is now only a wet-weather stream.

It is said that a peg-legged man named Frank Hawk drove a horse and buggy across before the present good-sized saplings were there to bar the way, and several people have been known to have ridden horses across. People have been coming to this strangely quiet and utterly beautiful place for over 150 years—and probably long before that.

POMONA
Natural Bridge

ROSCOE
M°ESELHORN

TOWER ROCK—Grand Tower

Tower Rock is a 60 foot high rock jutting out of the Mississippi at Grand Tower, Illinois. Only a small channel separates it from the Missouri shore. It is a federal site—the smallest one in the country. During Grant's administration a bridge was to have been built using the rock as a base. This never came to be, but the site has been federally protected since that time.

Marquette and Joliet recorded and described the rock. Mark Twain mentioned it in his *Life on the Mississippi*. It was used as a navigational checkpoint for riverboat captains for years and many boats ended their useful lives in the dangerous waters at its base.

The Indians believed evil spirits were always around the rock and throughout the Grand Tower area. There is the traditional Indian maiden legend concerning the rock. According to this legend a Fox Indian Maiden and a Wyandotte Brave leaped to their deaths rather than give up their love (as ordered to by a Fox Medicine Man).

Jefferson Memorial (headquarters of the St. Louis Historical Society) houses the pilot house of the *Golden Eagle* which sank at the base of the rock. River boats were often sunk, reclaimed, renamed and reused in the heyday of riverboats.

This was the third and last sinking of the *Golden Eagle* and it took the efforts of a St. Louis school teacher and her students to raise the funds to put the pilothouse in a place where other generations of children could see for themselves how the pilot house of a Mississippi riverboat looked.

The tiny town of Grand Tower is a true river town. Businessmen in a town such as this had a precarious existence, as the river could be counted on to rise and regularly flood them out. The Gearhart General Store was one of these local businesses and although Helen and Harry Gearhart (and their son) have been dead for many years, and their store boarded shut for over 50 years, it still stands sturdily beside the river in Grand Tower. You can still see where expensive lumber was provided for their son and his friends in order to keep them busy building clubhouses and to keep them from listening to the siren call of the river. Grand Tower locals called the Gearharts foolish—the Gearharts called it "survival". The Indians believed evil spirits were waiting down at the river. The Gearharts, although they didn't believe in evil spirits, knew that extreme danger was just outside their front door and they took what they considered necessary steps to avoid it.

TOWER
ROCK
GRAND TOWER
ILL.
Smallest Nat. Park

ROSCOE
MISSELHORN

The legend of the Piasa Bird is one of the oldest Indian legends and it is one that struck fear into all the Indians of the area. It was said to have regularly attacked the Indians and to have seized and eaten both adults and children—sometimes several per day. The Indians feared it with superstitious awe as an evil spirit.

The first recorded mention of the Piasa Bird was by Father Marquette on his 1673 voyage. Fathers Hennepin & Dousy & Gene Saint Cosme also mentioned it in 1699. Then there was no mention of it for over 100 years. According to the early written description of the painting it was really a petroglyph (shallow carving) painted red, green and black. It has generally been accepted as the greatest Indian Painting in North America.

Folklore indicates that the Indians set up a warning system to tell them when the evil bird was approaching. They posted scouts on the Mississippi where the view was good for many miles. Only the strongest and best swimmers were used as scouts because, if the Piasa Bird attacked, the scout would need to dive into the Mississippi and swim under water for lengthy periods of time.

Finally, Wassatoga, the young chief of the Illinois, in a dream vision fast, was told how to destroy the ''Bird of the Evil Spirit''. Young Wassatoga found a very prominent rock and made his sacrificial stand. As the giant bird swooped down to devour the young chief, his warriors were hiding in the nearby rocks. They waited, as they had been instructed, until the bird was very close. Then they sent their swift arrows into the red, green and black monster and the Piasa bird fell dead at the feet of the young Illinois chief.

The Indians commemorated this triumph over evil by painting a picture high on the cliffs along the Mississippi. Always after that time, as they passed the spot, they would loose arrows into the picture painted on the cliffs.

The ''original'' picture was quarried away for railroad ballast in 1847. A later one was reproduced from a sketch made in 1826. In 1870 another picture was destroyed and redone at a new site. The Boy Scouts finally took over the project of keeping the painting in good shape and in the 1980's instead of a short-lived painting there is a metal picture attached to the bluff face.

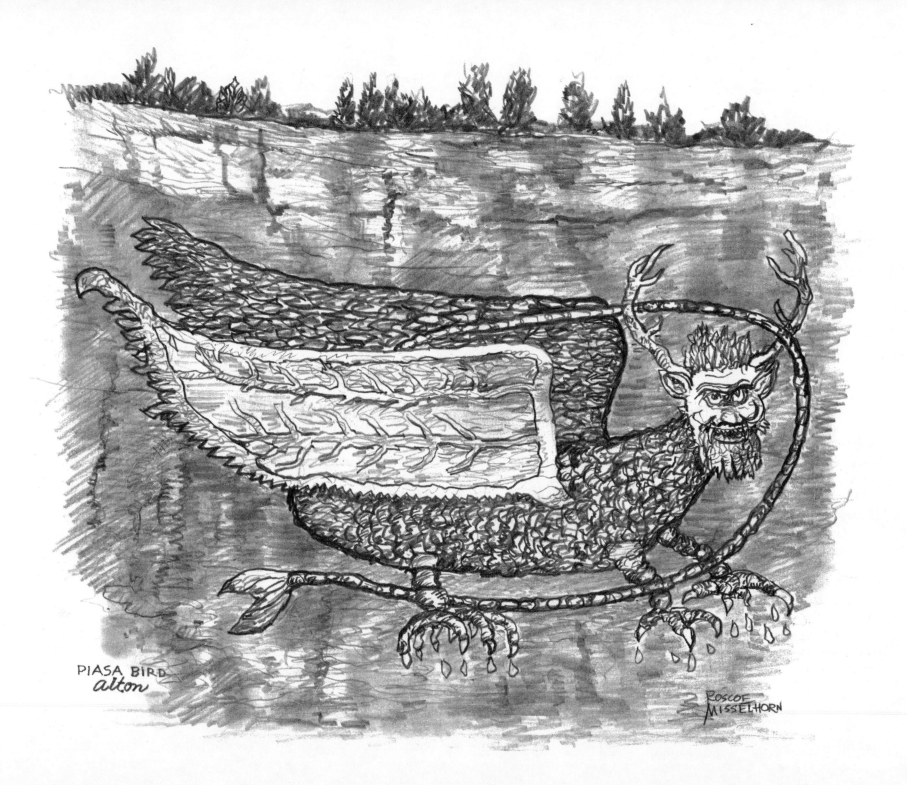

PIASA BIRD
alton

ROSCOE
MISSELHORN

LEWIS & CLARK HISTORIC SITE—near Hartford

The text of the plaque pictured reads: "Near here at Camp Dubois the Lewis & Clark detachment spent the winter of 1803-04. They left on May 14, 1804 and ascended the Missouri River to its source, crossed the Great Divide reaching the Pacific on November 7, 1805. They returned to Illinois on September 23, 1806, having concluded one of the most dramatic and significant episodes in our history."

The stone itself is a boulder from the spot in Montana where the Expedition crossed the Divide and for years was the only monument at the site (until the dedication of the new complex in September 1981). It is now surrounded by a circle of 11 three-sided concrete columns, one for each state along their trek and each bearing a plaque noting the important events of that state. The pylons also surround three flagpoles flying a replica of the 1804 flag, a current flag, and an Illinois flag. The columns and their ring-shaped roof stand atop a mound faced with limestone rip-rap, raised above any previously-known flood level and reached by a curving ramp. The circle opens to the northwest, and a giant arrow, recessed in the ground, points out to the mouth of the Missouri and its juncture with the Mississippi, the first step on the march. (The inset drawing is of the new monument.)

Preparations for the Expedition had been begun by President Jefferson even before the Louisiana Purchase of 1803, and this made possible the early start to explore and map the lands acquired. In fact, the Expedition beat the official news of the purchase to the area and, as a result, they could not camp at their first choice: LaCharrette, a settlement on the western side of the Mississippi. The Spanish commandant of the region, not having authorization, could not allow this "foreign" encampment on what he still had to regard as Spanish territory. And so the camp was located on the Riviere du Bois (the Wood River) on the eastern (Illinois) side of the Mississippi. The camp took its name from that river. Here William Clark (at 33, the oldest in the group) trained the 45 men and gathered supplies and equipment that 1803-04 winter.

The Expedition proceeded by keelboat and pirogue and then smaller craft up the Missouri to its source, transferred to horses for crossing the Divide, and built canoes for the trip down the Columbia River to the Pacific. The legendary Sacajawea joined the Lewis & Clark expedition early in 1805 before they left their wintering-over camp among the Mandan Indians in North Dakota. The information they sent back would be of incalculable importance in the opening of the West.

The present Historic Site (three miles north of Interstate 270, north of Oldenberg Road on Illinois Route 3, southwest of Hartford) is not the original camp site (that was claimed by the shifting waters of the rivers long ago). All three rivers have themselves changed location: the mouth of the Missouri is now south about two miles, the Wood River is north about one half mile, the Mississippi channel is east about one half mile. Yet today's site is the only conveniently accessible point of land from which one can see the meeting of the Missouri and the Mississippi as it must have looked to the Expedition then. Plans are to develop the area about it into a woodland park. When this is done, the site will evoke the look and feel of the original even more strongly.

LEWIS-CLARK
STATE MEMORIAL

In 1982 Cahokia Mounds became the tenth site in the United States to be named to UNESCO's World Heritage list. Listed as a site of "outstanding universal value to mankind" and "an exceptional testament to a vanished civilization," it has survived after decades of abuse, private exploitation, and neglect.

The area around Cahokia was the regional center of a vast prehistoric urban community which was served by satellite communities ranging as far as (present day) Dupo, Lebanon, Mitchell, East St. Louis and St. Louis. The site where Pierre Laclede instructed young Auguste Chouteau to establish the little fur trading post of St. Louis on the west bank of the Mississippi, was once entirely made up of these prehistoric mounds. A close look at the topography of Laclede's Landing (located at the north side of the "Arch") makes this readily apparent.

The present historic site preserves the central section of this prehistoric complex and is located between the Mississippi River's curve near East St. Louis and the Collinsville bluffs to the east. Now, as then, it is dominated by a great central mound known locally as "Monk's Mound" (named after a small colony of Trappist monks who resided there briefly in the early 1800's). This same central mound was the religious and ceremonial focus of the city which covered at least six square miles and whose population was in the tens of thousands—or perhaps much more. In its original prehistoric state the giant central mound was a great platform mound rising in four terraces to a height of 100 feet from its base of 14 acres. It was the largest Indian Mound north of Mexico and the largest prehistoric earthen construction in the new world.

There was no natural hill on the spot where the central mound was constructed. It was built entirely by human hands digging out soil from pits still to be seen in the area. And by carrying basketloads to be tamped and shaped in at least 14 stages over two centuries. It was topped, in its heyday, by a great thatch-roofed and clay-plastered pole building.

The Cahokia Mound area was the site of over 1200 years of human habitation from the prehistoric days before and during the late Woodland Culture (700 A.D.) through to the Mississippian Culture which emerged around 900 A.D. The prehistoric poeple who lived here built an empire and trade network that stretched from the sea coasts to the Great Lakes, and up into Canada. Then they went into a decline and, for reasons still unknown, the site was abandoned by 1500 A.D.

The Cahokia Indians, an Illini Tribe who had migrated into the area only shortly before French Explorers made the first European contacts in the late 1600's, gave their name to the site but could provide no information on their predecessors.

The present Cahokia Mound site is state owned and about 40 original mounds are preserved—dominated now, as then, by "Monk's Mound". Reconstructions have been made of part of one of the stockade walls that surrounded the central city from about 1150 to 1350 A.D. There is some speculation that the wall served to separate the "haves" (or royalty) who lived on the heights from the "have nots" or workers (slaves?) who lived in the vast urban surrounding area.

Also preserved are some of the posts of one of the "Woodhenges" (circular sun calendars probably used for ceremony coordination) and typical dwellings of the culture. An on-site museum has many exhibits and collections of items associated with the site. It also has plans for great future expansion in order to serve as a proper headquarters of a World Heritage Site.

The view in this drawing is from the late 1800's, when a Mr. T. Amos Hill had a house on top of the mound.

MONK'S MOUND

ROSCOE
MISSELHORN

EADS BRIDGE VIEW—East St. Louis

Through the arches of the Eads Bridge National Historic Site can be seen five other national sites—St. Louis Basilica—the Old Courthouse—Gateway Arch—Goldenrod Showboat—Laclede's Landing. And (looking six miles east) an International Historical site—Cahokia Mounds.

Many bridges have come and gone since Eads Bridge was officially opened on July 4, 1874 as the first bridge to span the Mississippi (in the St. Louis area). It stands as a living monument to James Eads and the unorthodox and highly debated methods he used in building the world's first steel-truss bridge. The bridge has an overall length of 6222 feet and consists of three spans. It is 54 feet wide and stands 55 feet above the water at high-water level. Eads was not only the designer of the bridge, he was also the promoter and builder. In fact, practical knowledge of the river, obtained as Eads worked the river as a salvage operator, gave him insights others did not have. A bridge design by Lucius Boomer was the heavy favorite among the scientific and business community until the Gasconade River bridge he had built five years previously collapsed and killed many of the commercial and political elite of the city. Calvin Chase (the old salvage partner of James Eads) was killed in the crash and after this disaster, Eads took a renewed interest in his own bridge design and campaigned forcefully to receive the bridge building bid. Fortunately for both East St. Louis and St. Louis, he was successful. The bridge was built (primarily to be used as a railroad bridge) for a cost of $10,000,000 and some of the construction methods invented by Eads (such as use of the diving bell) are still being used today. Lucius Boomer returned to Chicago from which city he had come.

Through the arches of the bridge can be seen the Gateway Arch—a later day international first. Eero Saarinen's design was chosen from among 200 entries in a 1947 national competition. Soaring 630 feet above the ground (75 feet higher than the Washington Memorial) it was an engineering problem that was not easy to solve—in fact construction was completely halted for one long period while engineers re-evaluated the entire structure. "Topping out" was in October 1965. Tourists by the millions come from all over the world to admire **The Arch.** Many of them take the ride to the top in one of the eight little five-passenger cars in each leg of the Arch. For their efforts, they see a spectacular view both up and down the river. For the less venturesome there is a wonderful museum of Westward Expansion under the Arch—and a most interesting movie that shows the entire building process.

At one time the banks on either side of the Mississippi were lined with riverboats. This romantic era, however, did not last long. (In the 1830's alone, there were more that 72 explosions claiming more than 600 lives). If the boats survived explosions, they were likely to flounder on snags and debris deposited by high water. Rivers were strewn with ruined hulls and sunken cargo. Railroads (and later modern highways) virtually changed the face of river traffic—and the fate of East St. Louis and St. Louis.

In this Misselhorn sketch of the St. Louis skyline (as seen from East St. Louis) you can see national monuments and riverboats. You can also see two places of interest to the Swiss Village Book Store, publisher of this book. The PET, Inc. building on the left originated with Pet Milk Company of Highland in 1885 (Highland is the Swiss town where the first Swiss Village Book Store originated in 1978). The St. Louis side of Eads Bridge ends beside the second location of the Swiss Village Book and Antique Store on Laclede's Landing.

EADS BRIDGE & ST. LOUIS

ROSCOE
MISSELHORN

MARINA TOWERS—Chicago

Marina Towers is a "City-within-a-city" residential and shopping complex. It houses 1300 and more persons in twin towers with parking on the first 18 stories and apartments the rest of the way up.

The most unusual feature of Marina Towers is the marina itself with mooring and storage space for 500 motorboats right in the heart of Chicago.

The design of Marina Towers was by Bertrand Goldberg. He designed it to be 588 feet high and on the top there is an observation deck. Circular apartment dwellings may have been built since, but these are said to be the first.

Chicagoans, as a whole, are now proud of Marina Towers but, in the past, they have been known to refer to them as "two corncobs standing on end".

MARINA TOWERS

ROSCOE
MISSELHORN

CORNER OF STATE & RANDOLPH—Chicago

For many years—dating back to the turn of the century—when Chicagoans made dates to meet downtown under "the clock", there was no question as to where that location was. It was the Marshall Field clock on State & Randolph in the area that was once said to be one of the busiest in the world.

"The clock" weighs almost eight tons and is of cast bronze. There are lights inside to help keep moisture out of the works and to illuminate the clock faces. It is powered by electricity and controlled and corrected by a master clock in the store that is itself corrected twice a day. When Norman Rockwell drew "the clock" on the cover of the *Saturday Evening Post* on November 3, 1945, it attained a classic national recognition.

The Marshall Field Company is one of the most famous department stores in the world. It was founded in 1881 by Marshall Field, who had begun his career as a clerk. He was often call the "Merchant Prince" of Chicago. The original building was located on the corner of Wabash & Washington, but soon expanded until the original store stretched to State & Randolph Streets.

Marshall Field has always been noted for its clocks as well as for its many extras. Extras such as corps of translators ready to serve as shopping guides, guides ready to conduct tours of the store, and gourmet lunches ready to be served to you in the Walnut Room under a seasonal three-story evergreen. There is also a 13 floor inner court with a five-story skylight Tiffany dome said to be made of 1,600,000 separate pieces of glass.

New shopping malls may also have Marshall Field Stores, but none can compare with the flagship store on Randolph and State.

STATE and RANDOLPH
Chicago CIRCA 1915

MARSHALL
FIELD

ROSCOE
MISSELHORN

WRIGLEY FIELD—Chicago

"Beautiful Wrigley Field," as the local slogan says, really is beautiful. And, on top of that, it was the site of one of the most legendary home runs ever hit by the game's most legendary player.

Wrigley Field started out as Weeghman Park. It was built in 1914 for the Chicago Whales of the Federal League (in a short-lived attempt to establish a third major league in baseball). When that circuit folded in 1916, the Whales' owner, Charles Weeghman (of Weeghman's Cafes, the Chicago lunchroom chain) was allowed to buy the Cubs, who had been organized back in 1876 and were in 1985 the only charter member left in the National League.

Most fans today do not realize the thanks still owed Weeghman, not just for moving the Cubs from their crumbling West Side Park to his new (and vacant) one on the Near North Side, but also for establishing a policy (new to baseball) of letting the spectators keep any ball hit into the stands.

The same year, 1916, Philip K. Wrigley's father bought into the team as well, and three years later he became the majority stockholder. Under father and son the original 14,000-seat Weeghman Park was expanded to the present 36,644-seat Wrigley Field. At the same time, certain things were not changed—there were still no billboards, no night lights, and no garish scoreboards.

While the absence of these modern "amenities" is becoming almost legendary itself, it still cannot hold a candle to the legend that sprang from the 1932 World Series game (third in the series, first in Chicago) that gave the sport a play that's been talked about ever since. For it was here in the fifth inning of a tie-game that Babe Ruth of the visiting Yankees (with two strikes on him and the hometown fans and dugout yelling derision) raised two fingers, pointed to the centerfield fence, and cracked the next pitch out of the Field and right through a high tree beyond. The tree was full of people who had been watching the game and they "rained out" of the tree to pursue what is said to have been the longest hit of the Field's history to that time.

Opinion is divided (and "The Babe" never told) but Joe Sewell's wife (Joe grounded out right before Babe) was sitting in the stands with Mrs. Ruth and she said it was "The Babe" keeping his promise to a kid in the hospital to hit a home run just for him. Others said he was just responding to the taunting Cubs and Cub fans. His hit would put the Yankees ahead to stay that game, but it also proved to be his last home run in a World Series. (And it is almost stirring enough to take Cub fans' memories off the fact that they lost not only that game but the series to the Yankees, who swept it in four.)

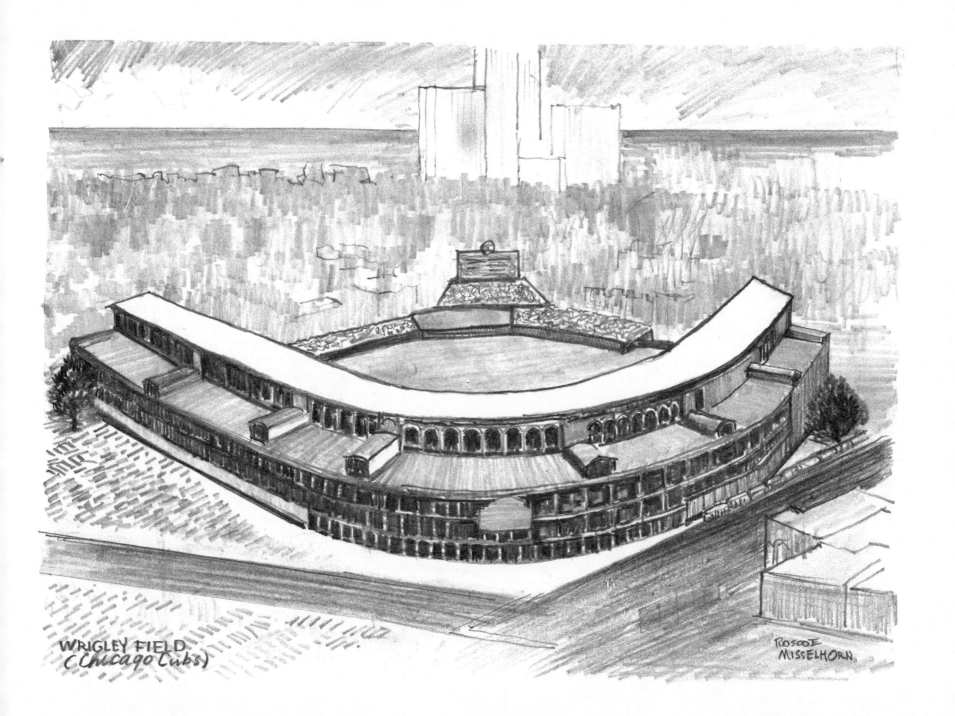

WRIGLEY FIELD
(Chicago Cubs)

ROSCOE
MISSELHORN.

ART INSTITUTE LION—Chicago

Pictured is one of the pair of lions that have been guarding the Michigan Avenue entrance of the Art Institute since 1895.

Art Institute roots go back to the Chicago Academy of Design (founded in 1866), one of the first art schools in the country. The Institute was formed in 1879 as the Chicago Academy of Fine Arts to provide instruction in, and promotion and exhibition of, the arts. It became the Art Institute of Chicago in 1882 (with the help of Marshall Field).

In 1893 Charles L. Hutchinson, the president of the Board of Trustees of the Institute and the head of the Fine Arts Committee of the Columbian Exposition, arranged for the Institute to advance sufficient funds for a permanent structure (rather than the temporary one first proposed) to be built here for the Congress of Religions to use during the World's Fair—and the Art Institute to use thereafter for its classes, collections, and other activities. It has occupied the site ever since, though the building has been enlarged and remodeled many times.

The Italianate Renaissance building was done by the same architectural firm that had done the Library of Congress in Washington. With its warm smoky-toned patina, it houses what is traditionally considered (and not just by Chicagoans) one of the greatest art collections in the world. There is an outstanding French Impressionist collection and more-than-representative works from every era of art and every area of the world. In addition, the Institute maintains the professional artists' school that was its beginning, a theater and dramatic school, a Junior Museum and Little Library. There is also a Young Artists Studio to promote an early appreciation of art, two other art libraries (one on architecture, one on the fine and decorative arts) as well as a schedule of lectures, film programs, and special exhibits.

The lions themselves were created by Edward L. Kemeys, a dentist-turned-sculptor, and were purchased by Mrs. Henry L. Field for the Museum. They guard the broad steps leading from Michigan Avenue to the main entrance and weigh three tons apiece. Long a favorite (and permitted) perch of both Chicago and visiting youngsters—as evidenced by the shine of their tails—each December they are proudly decked out in wreaths and red ribbons to share the holiday festivities.

ROSCOE
MISSELHORN

OLD WATER TOWER—Chicago

A sturdy survivor of fire, time, and modern growth, the old water tower of Chicago still stands as it has since it was built in 1867-69.

At the time of the great Chicago fire of 1871, its supposedly-fireproof pumping station was struck by flaming timbers and destroyed. Since this pumping station supplied all the mains on the north side of the city, destruction of that part of Chicago was insured.

The tower was built in Pseudo-Gothic style by architect William W. Boyington. The outside texture of the building is rough-faced, cream-colored limestone. Its crenellated battlements and turrets (and rebuilt pumping station) remain in place surrounded completely by modern city growth, but a constant reminder of the past.

OLD WATER TOWER

ROSCOE
MISSELHORN

"NEW" BANK—Shawneetown

Only two communities in the country were established by an act of Congress. They were (old) Shawneetown and Washington, D.C. Shawneetown was the oldest English settlement in Illinois, as it was surveyed and platted in 1810. It became famous as the gateway to Illinois. The nearby salt deposits were as important as the location, which was on the Ohio near the Wabash River mouth.

The John Marshall Bank was the first Shawneetown Bank. It was originally a house built in 1804. It was the first brick house in Shawneetown and it became the first bank in Illinois. As the first bank, it issued the state's first currency in 1816. It was forced to close in 1823 because of St. Louis competition, but it reopened in the 1830's.

The "new" Shawneetown bank was built in 1839 and is a Greek Revival structure. It has an imposing flight of steps and fine Doric columns. The portico of sandstone was brought down the Ohio River by flatboat from Eastern quarries. It cost $80,000— a huge sum in those days. A great future was predicted for Shawneetown at the time and such an expense did not seem unreasonable.

It is said that in the early days (when Shawneetown was the most important town in Illinois) some businessmen rode down to Shawneetown from the tiny settlement of Chicago. They requested a loan from the bankers of Shawneetown. The prudent bankers sent someone to investigate and evaluate the possibilities, and the loan was refused on the grounds that any village so far from Shawneetown could never amount to anything.

By 1937 constant flooding had driven most of the Shawneetown residents to higher ground and the original site became known as "old Shawneetown".

OLD SHAWNEETOWN BANK

ROSCOE
MISSELHORN

YACKLES FISH MARKET—Shawneetown

Located on the Ohio River in Shawneetown is the oldest continuously-operated fish market in middle America. At the time Roscoe Misselhorn did his original sketch of it, there was no new Shawneetown, and "old" Shawneetown was still being flooded out regularly each spring. With the help of W.P.A. labor, the main part of Shawneetown was moved to higher ground. But remaining in its original location was the Yackles Fish Market, still just two blocks from the old Shawneetown bank. Specialty: a very particular brand of catfish.

Roscoe Misselhorn found Yackles Fish Market a "very interesting" place to sketch, and his sketch of it is his favorite of all his work. From his initial sketch, he experimented and made his **first** wood-cut. It brought him his greatest claim to fame because The Library of Congress accepted the wood-cut for a traveling art show which was initially held in the Carnegie Institute and then was sent to every museum in the country. The catalog of the traveling show lists museums all across the country in which the Misselhorn wood-cut was put on display, and it is one of the proudest of Misselhorn's possessions. The fact that it was his **first** wood-cut merely underscores the artistic versatility of the extremely talented Roscoe Misselhorn.

YACKLES FISH MARKET

SHAWNEETOWN
ROSCOE
MISSELHORN

CAVE-IN-ROCK—Elizabethtown

Anyone who has ever seen the film *How the West Was Won* can never forget Cave-In-Rock—that Ohio River pirate lair where many people on their way west made their last earthly stop.

Located near Elizabethtown on the Ohio River the huge cavernous mouth of the cave was long a landmark for Ohio River boatmen—because of its high visibility—even from the far side of the river.

The cave is said to have been a center of Indian life in prehistoric times and to have been known to tribes in the area in the days of European exploration as "The Habitation of the Great Spirit," the cave of Manitou. First mentioned in 1729 as *Caverne dans le Roc* by M. de Lery, the site was first marked on a map in 1744 in Charlevoix's *History of New France*. Even before the end of the Revolutionary War, it had become widely known as a landmark and stopping place for explorers, trappers, boatmen and tradesmen taking cargo to New Orleans, pioneers on the way West, and also for rabble fleeing the more settled regions.

About 1797 Samuel Mason, a former Continental Army officer, occupied the site with a tavern for flatboat crews and erected the famous (or infamous) sign "Liquor Vault and House of Entertainment." He and his gang turned pirate, using the tavern as a front for their notorious operations. In 1803 Mason was killed by his own men for reward money, but the notoriety of the area continued.

In the early 1800's Micajah and Wiley Harpe (better known as "Big" and "Little" Harpe) based their gang there before moving on. Counterfeiters from Duff to Sturdevant operated on the site till 1831, and various other small gangs came and went until Federal troops were sent in 1834 and killed or drove out those remaining.

The cave is along the north bluff of the river, about midway up its face (varying, of course, with the level of the river, which has been known to flood the cave). It is distinguished by a graceful arch-opening 55 feet wide at its base and about 20 feet high. The cave itself extends about 200 feet into the bluff and has a small chamber branching right from the rear. The ceiling remains horizontal, but the floor slopes upward toward the rear. There is a sinkhole from the top of the bluff into the cave near its back down which one can see into the cave. Within the cave, one can see waterlines marking the depths/heights of various past floodings.

Now a State Park, the cave (and its notorious past) has been featured in films including *How the West Was Won* and Disney's television series *Davy Crockett and the River Pirates*.

CAVE-IN-ROCK

ROSCOE
MISSELHORN

OLD ROSE HOTEL—Elizabethtown

This old hotel ranked, until recently, as one of the oldest continuously-operated hotels in the midwest. It was the last of the once noted line of river hostelries. It has a wide veranda, a shady lawn overlooking the river, and a summer house which once served as a lighthouse to guide river traffic.

Old Rose Hotel was licensed in 1813 and was known originally as McFarland's Tavern. Captain James McFarland built the frame two-story building on a rocky point high above the Ohio River near the infamous Cave-In-Rock. Captain McFarland operated the ferry at the site from the year 1806, and the town which grew up at the spot was named after his wife Elizabeth.

McFarland's Tavern was a popular stopping spot for travelers—even after McFarland's death in 1830—when it was operated by others.

In 1884 a widow, named Sarah Rose bought the tavern and gave it its name—Rose Hotel. She operated the hotel until her death in 1939, after which time it was managed by her daughter (Mrs. Gullet).

The Old Rose Hotel ceased operation in the late 1970's, but remains standing as a proud monument to an illustrious past.

OLD ROSE HOTEL
on the OHIO
ELIZABETH TOWN

ROSCOE
MISSELHORN

OLD MAIN DOORWAY—Southern Illinois University—Carbondale

Through the pictured doorway of "Old Main" passed generations of young people from Southern Illinois. This doorway (for many years) held the key to the only higher education available to the people of Southern Illinois. It stood sturdily in place from its dedication in 1887 until it was destroyed by fire on June 8, 1969.

Chartered in 1869 as Southern Illinois Normal University, classes began in 1874. Its stated purpose was to train teachers. It remained within these narrow guidelines for many years. An accelerating curriculum brought about a name change to reflect its added dimension and in 1947 Southern Illinois Normal University became Southern Illinois University.

Good leadership has always been a trademark of this university which has continuously stressed the importance of improving the economic, educational, and cultural opportunities of the often neglected southern part of the state.

Under Delyte Morris, a man of great vision and political foresight, Southern Illinois University expanded to include the St. Louis metro area surrounding its strikingly beautiful Edwardsville campus.

OLD MAIN
CARBONDALE

ROSCOE
MISSELHORN

MAGNOLIA MANOR—Cairo

This beautiful home was the social center of Cairo during the late 1880's. It dates back to the days when great steamboats plied the Ohio and Mississippi Rivers and the leading riverport at the rivers' confluence was Cairo. Built in 1872 by Charles Galigher, the greatest day of Magnolia Manor was when ex-President and Mrs. Ulysses S. Grant were guests here upon their return from a world tour in 1880.

Now owned by the Cairo Historical Association, Magnolia Manor was built to withstand the damp river air of the Ohio and Mississippi Rivers which converge at Cairo. Magnolia Manor and many fine homes of this late 19th century era were built with double brick walls. The ten-inch insulation space between the bricks, however, may well be unique. Undoubtedly its presence must have improved the health of the occupants of this home located in the damp river region.

Magnolia Manor is a distinctly Southern style mansion located on the corner of 28th & Washington Streets. It is furnished with Victorian antiques and it still has some of the magnificent magnolias which gave it its name. Built for the great future envisioned for the southern part of the state, it stands as mute testimony to what might have been.

MAGNOLIA MANOR
CAIRO, ILL.

R. MISSELHORN

STEAMBOAT—Cairo

Steamboats were seen to be very romantic, but they were actually dangerous and were likely to explode or get caught on a snag and to sink on very short notice. The bottom of the Mississippi was littered with steamboat hulks. James Eads (of Eads Bridge fame) learned the ways of the river by operating a salvage company to retrieve some of these wrecks. In this capacity, he walked the bottom of the Mississippi thoroughly—he had to do it himself as he could find few men who would do it for him. Steamboats were always sinking, and being raised, and re-named again. This happened time after time. The *"Golden Eagle"* for example, when it sank at Tower Rock near Grand Tower, was on its third life. Of most danger were the races when boilers were stoked to the bursting point, and passengers cheered on the captains, and bets were placed on the outcome.

The first man to prove that a steamboat could go all the way from Pittsburg to New Orleans was Nicholas Roosevelt, who was a partner of Robert Fulton. He made the first trip in 1811 against totally unanimous predictions of failure—his brave young wife accompanied him (and had a baby along the way). He did not do this, however, without carefully taking almost two years to make the trip and check everything out in advance (also to set up fueling stations at what he considered reasonable stopping places). He must have had remarkable powers of persuasion because the people he convinced to set up fueling stations had never seen a steamboat and yet, when the boat arrived, they were on hand.

1811 was the year of Halley's Comet and it was a year of strange and violent weather. It was also the year of terrible floods and the mighty earthquakes which destroyed New Madrid and changed the face of the land. The "New Orleans" rode it out, but in after years his wife told how they often anchored to islands that were gone in the morning and how piteous refugees begged to be rescued from the destruction all around them and they had to steam right by them unable to help in such mass devastation.

Cairo, because of its location where the Ohio and Mississippi join, was an important stopping point for steamboats. This Misselhorn sketch was done in 1945.

GEORGE ROGERS CLARK STATUE—Fort Massac-Metropolis

This bronze figure commemorates the landing of George Rogers Clark and his 150 to 175 "Long Knives" east of the fort site on Massac Creek. Here they hid their boats and then marched overland to take Kaskaskia in 1778.

His capture of this and other French/British settlements along the Mississippi Valley in the name of the state of Virginia (and the newly-declared nation) was topped only by his 175-mile trek back across uncharted Illinois country to retake Vincennes. A cadre of his men had taken Vincennes earlier that summer only to have it retaken from them by the British in the fall. By the time Clark and his band (part Massac-originals and part Mississippi Valley-French volunteers) set out in February, there had been a freeze and a thaw, and they had to wade neck-high in the frozen waters of a flooding Wabash before completing their conquest of the "old" Northwest.

These victories gave the deciding advantage to the claims of the United States to not just the thirteen original colonies but also to the wilderness from the Appalachians to the Mississippi. All this they were ceded by the British in 1783. Clark, himself, received little reward for his patriotic exploits. He received a sword voted him by the Virginia legislature. His fame, however, endures and he is forever remembered as the father of the Northwest Territory.

Fort Massac itself was no deterrent to Clark for, by the time of his landing, it had long been in ruins. The last Ohio River fort erected by the French, it began as a trading post in 1702 and was only fortified in 1757, passing to the British at the close of the French and Indian War in 1763. The British did not take possession until 1765, and the fort burned that year and remained in ruins during the British occupation of the site. In 1794 George Washington, concerned with the possible threat from the Spanish holdings west of the Mississippi River, ordered it rebuilt by General "Mad Anthony" Wayne. It remained garrisoned until 1814.

Fort Massac has been called by a wild profusion (and confusion) of names: the Old Cherokee Fort, Fort Assumption, Fort Ascension (because it was dedicated on May 10, 1757: Ascension Day), Fort Massiac (from the French minister of the colonies who ordered its fortification: the Marquis de Massiac), Fort Massaic and Fort Massac (probably variant or mis-spellings of Massiac). Even Fort Massacre (romantically, because of the legends of Indian battles here). A great number of traditions, legends and "fairy tales" are associated with the site which has seen enough history (including the alleged Burr conspiracy) to fuel them all.

In 1903 the Daughters of the American Revolution raised money to purchase the site and (with the Illinois State Historical Society) campaigned for its restoration. In 1908 it became the first state park in Illinois, and in 1932 the statue by Leon Hermant was unveiled. Today it dominates the site of the reconstruction of the last American fort and the annual festival of colonial and military life of the 1700's held every October. Clark stands here, forever enshrined, gazing across the Ohio to where his great adventure began.

ROSCOE
MISSELHORN

PIERRE MENARD HOME—Kaskaskia

The French Colonial Style of the Pierre Menard home in Kaskaskia was reminiscent of the plantation homes of Louisiana. Designed by Joseph Champaigne, it was built in 1802 by slaves and was often referred to as the "Mount Vernon of the West".

Pierre Menard was presiding officer of the territorial legislature when it was part of the Illinois Territory and he was elected the first Lt. Governor when Illinois became a state. This required a special act of the legislature because Pierre Menard was not a native-born United States citizen. He had first arrived in the region as a French-Canadian fur trader. Two well-chosen marriages, plus a lot of native ability and wide experience, had considerably improved his lot in life.

The Pierre Menard home stands on a grassy bluff above the Mississippi and just north of the site of old Kaskaskia (which had to be moved). It is one story high and built long and low. The roof sweeps out over the long, columned porch. It is a clapboard covered frame structure resting on an exposed stone basement. A wide veranda, supported by large stone pillars, extends across the front and around the sides. Also on the grounds, is a stone kitchen connected to the house, a two-story brick smokehouse, and a stone springhouse.

In 1927 the site was acquired by the state and it became part of Fort Kaskaskia State Park. It contains some of the original furnishings and personal belongings of Pierre Menard and his family.

HOME OF
PIERRE MENARD

PIERRE MENARD
HOME
FT. KASKASKIA

ROSCOE
MISSELHORN

Founded in 1703 by the French on the west bank of its namesake river, the mission and trading center of Kaskaskia grew to become the largest of the French Mississippi settlements. Ceded to the British after the French and Indian War, the Kaskaskians burned their ungarrisoned fort rather that have it taken over. The British built a new one in its place and remained in command until it was captured by George Rogers Clark in a surprise attack in 1778. Kaskaskia continued to be the seat of civil and military authority in the new nation.

In 1809 Kaskaskia became the capital of the Illinois Territory and in 1818 reached a brief height as the first capital of the new state of Illinois. It was in Kaskaskia that the first constitutional convention met and drew up Illinois' first constitution, with a specially amended section that reduced the 30 years of United States citizenship required of the Governor, to citizenship and two years residence in the state for the Lieutenant-Governor. This allowed popular Pierre Menard, a citizen of Kaskaskia and a French-Canadian, to be elected the first Lieutenant-Governor of Illinois. Vandalia (a more central location) was also selected to replace Kaskaskia as capital, although the move could not be immediate.

In the building pictured (the two-story stucco and brick house of Dr. George Fisher built shortly after 1800), the first session of the General Assembly was held. The state rented three rooms for $4.00 a day. The 29 members of the House of Representatives and the 14 Senators met in low-ceilinged rooms that were also used as law offices. Governor Shadrach Bond found his Kaskaskia farm more attractive, but it was in Dr. Fisher's house that the legislature continued to meet until 1820 when the seat of government moved to Vandalia—the new capital. In 1820 all the paperwork of a state government could be moved in **one** oxcart.

This political blow to Kaskaskia was followed by a series of natural ones. A flood in 1844 damaged much of the town, drove many people and the county records (and eventually the county seat) a few miles downstream to the safety of its former commercial rival Chester. Then in the great flood in 1881 the Mississippi cut a new channel through the penisula above the village and made the Kaskaskia riverbed its own. Much of the village was inundated and swept away, and the rest was gradually washed away by the river. In a "spring freshet" in 1900, the double chimney of the former first capitol fell into the river. Some of the buildings, or parts of them, were salvaged and rebuilt in the new village in the center of what had become an island. And before waters could destroy their resting place, Governor and Mrs. Bond were removed and reburied in Chester.

Now the site of that bustling city of some 7000 people lies under the waters of the Mississippi. Its descendant, a village of some hundred people on an island that lies west of the river, is a small enclave of Illinois surrounded by Missouri.

Still remaining and keeping vigil is one last participant in the statehood celebrations of December 3, 1818 (when Illinois was proclaimed the 21st state and Kaskaskia its capital), the "Liberty Bell of the West". It is actually older than its Philadelphia cousin. The great bronze bell was originally cast in 1741 and sent by Louis XV to the French Mission here. It was rung when George Rogers Clark and his men captured the settlement on July 4, 1778. How it survived the flood a century ago prompts conjecture and conflicting theories, but survive it did and it "returned" to remain with the village and the island that continue the name of Kaskaskia.

FIRST CAPITOL of ILLINOIS
KASKASKIA, ILL.

ROSCOE
MISSELHORN

FIRST EXECUTIVE MANSION—Kaskaskia

From the house pictured, Shadrach Bond officiated as the first Governor of Illinois in its first state capital. At the time Kaskaskia was located on the west bank of the Kaskaskia River, about six miles east of the Mississippi (the two rivers joined some miles south of the village). In 1881 the flooding Mississippi moved from six miles west of town to scour a new channel north of the town. It took over the former Kaskaskia River channel and isolated the village on an island site. It gradually ate away whatever of the site had not been immediately inundated until the last vestiges went into the Mississippi around the turn of the century. Though there was time to remove some of the buildings (such as the Shadrach Bond home) to the "new" Kaskaskia (which was more securely situated in the center of the island), others went too quickly or had been too damaged to be saved.

Shadrach Bond, born in 1773 of a Maryland farming family, had immigrated to the "American Bottom" in the Illinois country in 1794. He lived here with his uncle, one of the first English-speaking settlers in the area. A point of some confusion enters here, for both uncle and nephew bore the same name (they are sometimes styled "the elder" and the "the younger" or "Sr." and "Jr.", respectively). They were contemporaries for some years and were both politically inclined. "Our" Shadrach Bond moved to his own farm on the bank of a lake in the area and liked to ride to the hounds. A large man (six feet tall and about 200 pounds) he had a dignified and commanding bearing, he was intelligent, practical, and honest—a man of the common people.

SHADRACH BOND MONUMENT—Chester

Bond served in the legislature of the Indiana Territory in 1807 before Illinois attained separate territorial status in 1809. He was elected to Congress as the first representative of the Illinois Territory in 1812. Before his return to Kaskaskia, Bond was appointed receiver of public moneys in the Land Office there. About the same time he took up this post, he moved to a farm nearer the village.

In 1818 (when Illinois became a state) he was elected governor, having run unopposed for that office. His governorship saw two state capitals and he presided at both. In December 1820 he was in Vandalia to open the General Assembly in its new (second) capitol. While there he lived with his brother's daughter and her husband (Robert and Isabella Bond McLaughlin) in a simple two-story white frame house, and he entertained with the same hospitality and generosity he displayed at home in Kaskaskia. It was to Kaskaskia that he returned after his term, and though he remained influential in the state, he was not successful thereafter in his campaigns for other public offices. He died in 1832 and was buried, with his wife Achsah, in the Kaskaskia cemetery.

The 1881 flood that (eventually) destroyed Old Kaskaskia threatened the cemetery-site as well. In April of that year the Bonds' remains were removed and taken to the Evergreen Cemetery in Chester where they were re-interred in a vault. The state erected a monument on the site: a tall, white marble shaft that indicates this state memorial is the final resting place of Illinois' first governor.

The Governor and Mrs. Bond rest at the summit of a hill overlooking (but safely out of reach of) the Mississippi.

FIRST EXECUTIVE MANSION IN ILL.
GOV. BOND
KASKASKIA ILLS.

R. MISSELHORN

BOND

ELIAS KENT KANE HOUSE—Riley's Lake

There is something about Elias Kent Kane that seems forever just-out-of-reach, as shrouded by the mists of time as this house and Riley's Lake itself are. We remember him as our first state senator.

One can list his accomplishments and even hint at his maneuvering and politicking, yet cannot touch the man himself—a characteristic of his that has itself been noted by authors and historians.

Kane was of a distinguised New York family, a cousin of Chancellor James Kent, the noted United States jurist of the time, and a relative of Elisha Kent Kane, the 19th century Arctic explorer. A graduate of Yale, he had practiced law in Tennessee before coming out to Kaskaskia in 1814 as a young lawyer of about 20—"to seek his fortune" as had so many others in this capital of the Illinois Territory. He served as a United States District Judge shortly before Illinois' admission to the Union, and while he was actively involved in securing that admission.

As a delegate from Randolph County to the first Constitutional Convention held in Kaskaskia, he was much-respected and listened-to by the other 33 delegates (a tremendous gathering for the time). It was almost double what the membership of the first legislature here would be and more than Bennett's Tavern (the only stopping place) could handle. He is (and was even in his time) regarded as the virtual author of Illinois' first constitution and is said to have written much of it even before they convened early in August of 1818. During the convention he dominated the proceedings by serving on important committees and by negotiating compromises such as the capital-relocation issue (keeping it in Kaskaskia until the legislature could determine another site)

and the issue of slavery. Kane (himself a slaveholder) drafted a section promising the eventual dissolution of slavery and the indenture system which was probably essential to the admittance of Illinois to the Union. The constitution, a document of eight articles, was adopted by the delegates in 21 days and became effective upon Congressional approval.

The first election was held the next month and saw Shadrach Bond elected first Governor. He appointed Kane to be first Secretary of State, knowing he would need the assistance of such a literary and legally-trained man. In this position Kane served as the "power behind the throne," handling much of the Governor's work for him and drafting Bond's opening message to the first General Assembly.

Kane served as a member of the Illinois General Assembly. He became involved in various internal squabbles and was among the pro-slavery elements that sought (unsuccessfully) to call a constitutional convention to amend the slavery provisions of his original text.

He served two terms as a United States Senator, being elected in 1824 and re-elected in 1830. In December of 1835 he died while in Washington, D.C. His death was apparently much-lamented by the Congress and the people of Illinois (Kane County, established in January of 1836, was named after him) and his career seemed all the more conspicuous for its brevity.

Riley's Lake (sometimes Reily Lake) is named for the last owner of the grist mill that once had supplied Old Kaskaskia and French troops in the French and Indian War. It had been in operation since about 1722 and remained so until about 1855, 20 years after Kane's death. Kane is buried in what is now Fort Kaskaskia State Park.

Elias Kent Kane
HOUSE   Feb. 1980
Riley's Lake, Ill.

ROSCOE
MISSELHORN

STATEHOUSE—SECOND CAPITOL—Vandalia

Illinois was one of the five states created from the old Northwest Territory and, when it became a state, Vandalia was picked to be the first state capital over Kaskaskia (which had served as capital up to that time). It remained the capital for nearly twenty years until the capital was moved permanently to Springfield in 1837 by legislative decision.

In the Old Statehouse in Vandalia was issued the city charter of Chicago and here young Lincoln arrived in 1834 as a neophyte legislator. He had a $200 loan to tide him over while he went about acquiring his early legislative education.

The original Vandalia statehouse was destroyed by fire in 1823 and a second building was erected in 1824. In 1836 the second capitol was torn down because it was too cramped in space. Salvage from the second building was used in building the third. A desire to make the capital more centrally located led to the hotly contested move to Springfield. It has been said that Lincoln (who favored Springfield) once climbed out a window in order that a quorum of pro-Vandalia legislators capital site—(his presence would have constitued that could not vote on the capital site—(his presence would have constituted that quorum). Whether or not this is absolutely true is difficult to ascertain, but every visitor to the Old Statehouse hears this story.

In 1839 the state donated the Old Statehouse to Fayette County for courthouse purposes and it was used as such for many years. The present building is the fourth capitol, modified. It is two stories high and built of white brick of simple Greek Revival design: there was littel adornment until eight Doric columns (four brick on each portico) were erected in 1859. The main entrance was protected by a two-story galleried porch with slender arceded posts. Above the gabled roof is a cupola. The Upper Room at the western end has ten long benches, a semicircular railing and rostrum. These are all original pieces.

The Vandalia Courthouse is open to the public and, as an added attraction, on the courthouse ground there is the famous statue dedicated to the pioneer women of America because Vandalia was located on the old "National Trail".

SECOND STATE CAPITOL
VANDALIA

ROSCOE
MISSELHORN

OLD STATE CAPITOL—Springfield

The Old Restored State Capitol in Springfield owes its very existence to Abraham Lincoln—the state favorite son. It was Lincoln's persistence (as one of the "Long Nine") that moved the capital from Vandalia to Springfield and so gave birth to this statehouse. Here he served in the state office and delivered (in the Hall of Representatives) his "House Divided" speech; here he used the Governor's office as President-elect before leaving for Washington, D.C.; and here he was returned to lie in state after his death.

The building's cornerstone was laid July 4, 1837, though it was still unfinished in the fall of 1839 when the capital was formally moved and Springfield became the third capital of Illinois. The statehouse was occupied from 1840 but not finished until 1853, nearby churches having to serve as assembly rooms for the legislature as needed until then. With the construction of the "new" state capitol (ca. 1869), this building was deeded to Sangamon County, though there was an extended change-over period of office-movement. By 1895 the county government needed more room so the building was elevated and another story was constructed **beneath** it. The reconstructed county courthouse opened in 1901.

Built in Greek Renaissance style of native sandstone with rotunda, porticos and dome, this was the most impressive capitol in the (then) West: with the possible exception of Iowa's State Capitol built in Iowa City in the 1840's by the very architect (John R. Rague of Springfield) who had supervised construction of the Illinois capitol. The resemblance between the two was the first between these two state capitols, for the situation would be repeated at the time of construction of Springfield's second capitol.

The old capitol building was restored around the time of the state's Sesquicentennial celebration in 1968 and now houses the Illinois Historical Library. It has various Lincoln memorabilia (including one of the five copies of the Gettysburg Address in Lincoln's handwriting) and is the site of an impressive sound-and-light show on the major events in Lincoln's life.

ILLINOIS STATE CAPITOL—Springfield

Currently being considered for inclusion on the National Register of Historic Places, and with its "current" remodeling now going into its second decade, the latest Illinois State Capitol continues the tradition of change and controversy common to its ancestors.

Begun in 1868 to replace the earlier (first-in-Springfield, fifth-in-the-state) capitol building, the present statehouse was not completed until 1887 though government offices began occupation of the building in 1876 and continued to move in as accomodations became available.

The Renaissance-style structure is built in the form of a Latin cross, has 17-foot thick native limestone foundation walls, polished granite porticos, a tall dome and an elaborate interior, floored and wainscotted with many varieties of marble. It houses the Senate and House chambers and the Governor's office. Statues of Illinois' famous sons (and sometime-combatants) Lincoln and Douglas stand at the Second Street entrance of a building neither lived to see.

The original design is said to have been that of a Chicago architect but Alfred Piquenard, a French emigre, was supervising architect at the time of his death in 1876. He left, not only Illinois' Capitol an unfinished shell, but also Iowa's in about the same condition. He was overseeing the design and construction of both buildings at the same time, and apparently from the same basic plans, for they retain a strong similarity to each other.

Even before its completion, the building was undergoing change: the original plan of the front included a grand stairway leading up to a pillared portico, but in 1886 the then-architect tore out the stairs (already in place) and erected the pillars of the present structure.

And the changes continue apace.

STATE CAPITOL
SPRINGFIELD

ROSCOE
MISSELHORN

MAIN GATE OF ILLINOIS STATE FAIR—Springfield

The Main Gate of the Illinois State Fair is remembered by millions of people who have passed through to visit one of the great fairs in the United States. The Main Gate entrance was built in 1910 and was completely restored and re-lighted in time for the 1985 fair. The 1985 State Fair was the one hundred and thirty-third (133) edition of this annual event.

One of the distinguishing features that highlights the Illinois State Fair, and sets it apart from the other fairs, is the increasing international flavor. Exhibits from Australia, China, Japan, and many other countries add flair to this midwest attraction. In addition to these exhibits, many other nationalities are represented in the food and entertainment sections.

The Illinois State Fair has something for everyone, including entertainment, politics, free concerts, sports events, good food, agricultural and craft exhibits, and most of the other events and activities you would find at any good fair.

The big day at the Fair is, of course, Governor's Day. On this day the governor and his family appear and mingle with the voters.

ILLINOIS STATE FAIRGROUNDS. CIRCA 1914

ROSCOE
MISSELHORN

MISSELHORN'S MELANCHOLY LINCOLN

Abraham Lincoln was born on February 12, 1809 in a log cabin in Hardin (now Larue) County, Kentucky. Lincoln had an older sister who died in childbirth when Lincoln was a teenager, and a younger brother, Thomas, who died in infancy. Abraham Lincoln's grandfather Lincoln had been killed by Indians in 1786. Because of this tragedy his father, Thomas Lincoln, grew up as an illiterate wanderer. It was from his mother (who died when Abraham was very young) and later from his stepmother that Lincoln received encouragement in his efforts to learn.

Difficulty with land titles in Kentucky caused the family to move to Indiana in 1816 when Lincoln was seven years old. The family settled near Little Pigeon Creek in Perry (now Spencer) County. Lincoln recalled it as a constant fight with unbroken forest. It was in Indiana that Lincoln's mother (Nancy Hanks Lincoln) died in 1818. Lincoln was only nine years old. The following year Abraham and his sister found a ''good and kind mother'' in Sarah Bush Johnson, a Kentucky widow who married Thomas Lincoln.

When Lincoln was 21 years old, the Lincolns left Indiana for Illinois. This time they established a farm north of Decatur. Lincoln left home the next year and went to live in New Salem. It was here that he tried various occupations until he found what he liked best. Early into his New Salem years, he did a brief stint of service in the Black Hawk War. He was elected captain of his volunteer company and this distinction changed the direction of his life. He ran for Illinois legislature in 1832. He was unsuccessful the first time but he used the time in New Salem to good advantage as he studied law. Two years later he was elected to the lower house for the first of four successive terms as a Whig. Slavery, he felt, was the opposite of the American system of opportunity, and he publicly stated his opposition to it by the time he moved to

Springfield in 1837 to establish his law practice in the more promising (for a new lawyer) town.

Lincoln was always subject to deep spells of melancholy (or depression as it is called today). It was during one of these times that he was to have married Mary Todd (a refined Kentucky lady). Lincoln, reportedly, failed to appear for the wedding. Eventually, however, they did marry on November 4, 1842. To this marriage were born four sons: Robert Todd (1843-1926), Edward Baker (1846-1850), William Wallace (1850-1862) and Thomas (Tad) (1853-1871).

The only home Lincoln ever owned was in Springfield and it was from Springfield that Lincoln was elected President. By his inauguration in March 1861, seven states had already seceded from the Union. By April 12, 1861 South Carolina had fired on Fort Sumter and the Civil War had begun. In carrying on the war, Lincoln always looked for a general who would fight no matter what his politics were. He found one in Ulysses S. Grant. Lincoln was always interested in military campaigns and when he died, a copy of General Sherman's orders for the March to the Sea was found in his pocket.

September 22, 1862 Lincoln issued the Emancipation Proclamation by which all slaves were freed. In the election of 1864 (which many thought Lincoln would cancel because of the war) Lincoln endorsed the thirteenth amendment to the constitution abolishing slavery, whereas McClellan pledged to return to the South the rights it had had in 1860. Lincoln's election was a severe blow to the south.

On April 14, 1865 (five days after Robert E. Lee's surrender to Grant) Lincoln was shot and killed by John Wilkes Booth as he was attending a performance at Ford's Theatre in Washington.

ROSCOE
MISSELHORN

FLATBOAT—Lincoln's First Job

Abraham Lincoln, pushed, poled, and floated many flatboats such as this before he came to New Salem. He had made the trip downriver to New Orleans more than once and the strength he had developed in his arms served him well in the pioneer communities, where physical strength could well be the greatest asset a man could have.

When the Lincoln family moved from Indiana to Illinois in 1830, Abraham went with them although he was 21 years old. He resumed his flatboating trade on the Sangamon River and it was when his flatboat ran aground at New Salem that he made his first acquaintence with the people who lived there. He liked them, and when he felt it was time to establish independence from his father—and to leave home—it was to New Salem he came.

Before steamboats made their appearance, rivers were navigated by flatboats, keelboats and barges. They carried all the freight because no other transportation was available. The keelboat was sharp at the front and back and was long and slender. It was poled upstream by boatmen. When the keelboat had a low lengthwise house on it, it became a barge. In the pecking order of boats, a flatboat ranked dead last. It was built like an unwieldy box and was broken up for the lumber it contained when it arrived at its place of destination. It did, however, float upon water and it was used as a vehicle for transporation. It was also usually built from tall poplar trees found on the "old home place" and did not require sophisticated skill to build. Since the people of the West knew of nothing any better, they were satisfied with this method of transportation.

LINCOLN—BERRY STORE—New Salem

Lincoln left home to strike out on his own when he came to New Salem. From 1831 to 1837 (from age 22 to 28) New Salem was his home. (His first acquaintance with the town came about when his flatboat ran aground nearby). It was here that he clerked in a store, served as postmaster and deputy surveyor, enlisted in the Black Hawk War, failed in business, and was elected to the Illinois General Assembly in 1834.

New Salem was to have been a big town when it was first planned in 1827. But this growth was dependent upon improving the channel for year-round river traffic on the Sangamon River, and funds for improving the channel never materialized. The Post Office moved to Petersburg in 1836 and in 1838 Sangamon County subdivided, creating Menard County with Petersburg as a seat. New Salem continued to decline and was abandoned.

In 1906 William R. Hearst bought the site. He put it in trust of the Old Salem Chautauqua Association in 1919. From there title passed on to the Old Salem Lincoln League. It is now one of the most popular state parks in the state of Illinois.

At the present time about thirteen homes, shops, mills and taverns have been redone and furnished in the style of the 1830's. The Lincoln-Berry Store, where young Lincoln failed as a businessman, is one of the most visited of the restored sites.

R. MISSELHORN
7/3/47

BERRY-LINCOLN STORE

LINCOLN-BERRY STORE

OLD GRIST MILL—New Salem

Lincoln's New Salem was actually founded on this mill. James Rutledge and John M. Cameron platted the town site in 1829 with a two-fold hope of profit: from the sale of the lots and from an established and ever-increasing demand for the services of their saw and grist mill, located on the Sangamon River.

With the mill as a base, the town then attracted the other "middle-man" business enterprises that made it a trading center. New Salem, as it turned out, would not grow to become one of these larger cities and would not even be able to maintain this level for long. Its people would move on, to try again elsewhere.

Rutledge was prominent in New Salem and was the organizer of an early debating society, but he is better remembered as the father of Ann Rutledge who Abraham Lincoln would love and lose (by death) during his years here.

It was the Old Grist Mill (or, more specifically, its dam) that led to Lincoln's decision to settle in New Salem. It was on this dam in 1831 that his flatboat got stuck. He and his cousin and stepbrother had built it for Denton Offut and were navigating down the Sangamon to the Illinois, the Mississippi, and New Orleans when the accident happened. It was Lincoln's ingenuity and skill at getting the boat safely free that convinced Offut to hire him to clerk in his New Salem store (when he had returned from New Orleans some months later). So Lincoln came to New Salem to stay for the most formative and pivotal six years of his life.

The next year he had yet another, though less well-known, adventure with the same milldam. Springfield businessmen hoped to establish a river trade-route between their city and the Illinois River traffic via the Sangamon. To prove the feasibility, they had a 95-foot steamboat, the *Talisman,* come up from Cincinnati to Beardstown and then proceed up the Sangamon. The *Talisman* got safely past New Salem on its way up, because the river was in flood and the boat could clear the dam. But, by the time it reached Portland Landing, the river was falling and the pilot of the ship deserted. The captain decided not to attempt to continue any closer to Springfield (this would remain the nearest a steamboat ever came to it). It was necessary to hire someone who knew the river well enough to get the *Talisman* back downstream. This turned out to be a combination of Rowen Herndon and Abraham Lincoln—Herndon had piloted a ferryboat and so he steered the *Talisman*. Lincoln (who knew the river from his flatboat trips) pointed out the channel as they went. But by the time they reached New Salem, the river level was already so low that part of the mill-dam had to be dismantled for the boat to squeeze through on its way to the Illinois. It finally reached its goal three weeks later. The original *Talisman* burned shortly thereafter while docked at Alton. But its namesake (the first steamboat to attempt the Sangamon again) plies the river around New Salem today giving people a tour, in season, of the river Lincoln knew.

And the Old Grist Mill, whose rotting relics were excavated by state engineers in order to determine the exact location and size of the structure, stands today reconstructed on the Sangamon River in the New Salem State Park.

GRIST MILL
New Salem, Ill

ROSCOE
MISSELHORN

ABRAHAM LINCOLN HOME—Springfield

This house was the only one ever owned by Abraham Lincoln. He and his wife Mary (and their young son Robert Todd) moved into this house after two years of living in boarding houses. It was bought in 1844 for $1500 cash and a mortgage of $900.

Originally the house was a one and one-half story house, but in 1856 Mary had it raised to a full two stories. Some sources say this was done during one of Lincoln's circuit-riding sessions, and he didn't immediately recognize it on his return to Springfield.

Three of Lincoln's four sons (Edward, William, Thomas) were born in this house. Except for Lincoln's term in the United States Congress in 1847, when the house was rented out, the family lived here until they left for the White House in 1861. It was rented, thereafter, until 1887 when Robert Todd Lincoln deeded it to the State of Illinois.

The exterior is in Greek Revival style but with ornamental features. The green-shuttered white frame house has delicate trim and cornices; framework of white oak; lathes and weather-boarding of hand-split hickory and siding, trim and flooring of black walnut. Most of the construction used wooden pegs, the few iron nails being hand-wrought. It sits on a slight elevation, partly surrounded by a brick retaining wall and a white picket fence of unusual design that was built to Lincoln's order.

There is no great change in the interior, but most of the original furniture was destroyed in the Chicago Fire of 1871. When the Lincolns moved to Washington in 1861, they sold the furnishings to a tenant who moved with the furnishings to Chicago. Only a few of the personally-owned Lincoln pieces remain, including the President's desk, horsehair sofa and rocker, a secretary, hatrack, chest of drawers, shaving mirror, and a dessert service. The rest of the furnishings have been restored from the homes of friends and relatives of the period.

Here, a few blocks from the city's center and only a few blocks (then) from the surrounding farms, Lincoln pursued his career in law and politics, reared his family, and recieved word of his election to the Presidency.

Lincoln is buried in Oak Ridge Cemetery in Springfield. The visitors' register there shows the reverence with which Lincoln is held worldwide. There is seemingly no place in the world where Lincoln is unknown.

He is America's best known and most revered native son. "He belongs to the Ages."

ABRAHAM LINCOLN HOME
SPRINGFIELD, ILL.

ROSCOE
MISSELHORN

LINCOLN-DOUGLAS DEBATE MONUMENT—Jonesboro

In 1858 Lincoln was nominated to run against Stephen Douglas for the U.S. Senate. He accepted the honor with a speech in which he said "A house divided against itself cannot stand. I believe this government cannot endure permanently half slave and half free". He challenged Douglas (who favored slavery) to a series of debates over the slavery issue. Douglas accepted and named seven places. The first was in Ottawa on August 21, 1858. The last was at Alton on October 15. All the debates were attended by huge crowds except one. That one was the third held in Jonesboro on September 15, 1858.

A stone marker indicates the site in a 22-acre park maintained by the United States Forest Service. The debate was held at what was then the fairgrounds because the county fair was then in progress and fair time has always been a traditional time for politicians to meet with their constituents.

The setting for the debate was simple. A crude platform of rough planks was laid across logs in the shade of large trees. There was no bunting, no flags, and no rostrum for the speakers, just a large table for press secretaries to take notes. Planks across logs comprised seating arrangements. Some people brought household chairs from nearby houses or from wagons. The crowd of about 100 people was overwhelmingly favorable to Douglas. And, indeed, Douglas went on to win the Senatorial election of 1858, but the debates had brought Lincoln to national attention and made a strong impression on many influential Eastern Republicans. Lincoln went on to become President in 1861.

OLD SLAVE HOUSE—(Hickory Hill Mansion)—Equality

Salt was an important commodity in pioneer days and Hickory Hill Mansion was built in 1834 above the Saline River Valley because of the nearby natural salt springs. This salty mud made the area a haven for wild game. Indians had also frequented this area but their presence was no longer a threat.

John Hart Crenshaw, who arrived in the region in 1830, built Hickory Hill and became an important landowner (30,000 acres) because he controlled the saltworks. Hickory Hill Mansion (know to this day as the Old Slave House) was built in Greek Parthenon style with large wooden columns, each turned from an entire tree trunk. These served as supports for the second story porch and roof.

Salt was so important a product that the federal government allowed saltworks employers and owners to import leased slaves from the South to work wells and furnaces. Crenshaw used this privilege to its fullest extent. He was reputed to have "neglected" to free indentured servants as required and to have kidnapped free blacks for work or for sale.

The first and second floors of the house were used by the Crenshaw family but there is a third floor of the Old Slave House. It is reachable only by a steep narrow stairway and is divided into a number of small rooms and what appear to be tiny cells running on either side of a long central hall stretching north and south across the building. There is an underground entrance with access to this stairway and it is probable that slaves were herded to and from the salt mines using this entrance and that they were housed on the third floor. Iron rings were at one time attached to the floor and there were also two strange looking racks. Tales of hauntings and strange sounds abound, and many visitors have testified that, no matter how hot the summer day, the third floor of the Old Slave House remains cold and forbidding.

A scale model of this house is the property of the Swiss Village Book Store (publisher of this book).

OLD SLAVE HOUSE
EQUALITY. ILL.

ROSCOE
MISSELHORN
APR. 6 '45

UNDERGROUND RAILROAD (Burlingame House)—Eden

The Underground Railroad was a term used for hidden escape routes by which runaway slaves sought freedom in Canada or in northern states. Given the secrecy essential during its operation, a complete history of the Underground Railroad will probably never be known. There were so many stations run by so many people on so many lines all feeding North at irregular intervals from the "Free State-Slave State" interface that ran from the Atlantic seaboard to Kansas, it almost boggles the imagination.

Some of the individuals, places and routes in Illinois that are remembered include: William Reddick's mansion in Ottawa, a stop on at least one way North; Owen Lovejoy's home in Princeton, considered practically the divisional headquarters of the Underground Railway and one of the most important "stations"; and the Burlingame House in Eden, a village adjoining Sparta.

Burlingame House was a station on the line that began at Rockwood (then called Liberty) in Randolph County and extended through Carlyle. Runaway slaves coming across the Mississippi from Missouri were hidden at the farm of a Mr. Clendennig, north and east of Rockwood, and then taken, usually at night, to Eden and the home of a Mr. Burlingame, who operated a shop that made, among other things, farm pumps. Pumps that would be taken by wagon to market. The Carlyle region was such a good market that loads were regularly sent in that direction. As the round trip from Eden could not be made in one day, they, of course, had to take along feed for the horses or oxen that pulled the wagon. This was carried in a wagon box (about three feet wide, nine-to-ten feet long and two feet deep) that carried "passengers" as well.

The cargo was arranged so: the wagonbox would be loaded with its feed and its human cargo, well-hidden beneath hay or fodder, then the pumps and their long sections of log-pipe would be laid carefully lengthwise on top of the wagon. The driver would proceed to Carlyle where he would deliver his "passengers" to the local "station agent" and his pumps as usual, afterward returning to Eden.

As with so many of the routes the number escaping along this particular line, considered alone, was not large but became significant when combined with all the others in the Railway system. It played its part in getting an estimated 75,000 slaves to Canada and freedom.

apr. 10 66

UNDERGROUND SLAVE RAILWAY

ROSCOE
MISSELHORN

GENERAL JOHN ALEXANDER LOGAN MONUMENT—Murphysboro

This bronze equestrian statue, which stands on the grounds of the old high school in Murphysboro, was done by Leon Hermant.

John "Black Jack" Logan (called this because of his dark good looks) was a Civil War hero. He was at Vicksburg and was appointed military governor upon its capture. He was a political man having taken part in the Lincoln Presidential campaign and was himself nominated for Vice President on the ticket with Blaine in 1884. He was in the Illinois legislature and the United States Senate and was considered a gifted orator. He was a lawyer and was one of the managers of the impeachment proceedings against Andrew Johnson. He was an author of several books about the Civil War and about his life and service. He is probably best known for establishing the Grand Army of the Republic, a veterans organization made up of Civil War Veterans. He set up the first Decoration Day in honor of the War dead.

In his wife, General Logan had a brilliant and loyal helpmate. She was an author and writer and her book about life in Washington, as she saw it during their years there, was a best seller of its day.

The Sally A. Logan Library of Murphysboro does honor to the Logan family as the library was for many years housed in the Logan Family Home on Walnut Street. This was the family home and it was set aside for a library by her will.

JOHN A. LOGAN   MARY S. C. LOGAN

ERECTED BY THE PEOPLE OF ILLINOIS

GEN. LOGAN MONUMENT
Murphysboro

ROSCOE
MISSELHORN

FIRST DECORATION DAY—Woodlawn Cemetery—Carbondale

It is generally accepted that the honor of having held the first organized, community-wide observance of Decoration Day belongs to Carbondale's Woodlawn Cemetery. General John A. Logan was the speaker at this first day of remembrance that we now know as Memorial Day. Originally begun after the Civil War as a placing of flowers on the graves of the war dead, it was thereafter expanded to include the dead of all wars and the civilian dead as well.

Carbondale's claim to the honor of being first is supported by records kept by Mr. Green, caretaker of the town's early cemetery; accounts by the participants; and contemporary church records. The observance was held at Woodlawn Cemetery on April 29, 1866, the outgrowth of a similar but more spontaneous observance held at Crab Orchard Christian Church nearby earlier that month.

It was apparently the first in which returned veterans were major participants both in directing and in taking part. The promotion was in their hands and the events of the day set a pattern that was followed thereafter: a line of march (with 219 marching, led by Colonel E.J. Ingersoll, "Master of the Day"); prayer (offered by Reverend J.W. Lane, pastor of the First Methodist Church); speeches (General John A. "Black Jack" Logan, speaker of the day); decoration of graves (of the Civil War dead only) including one unknown soldier; there was a barbeque; and one fight.

There is a bronze marker at the cemetery entrance to mark the occasion and place.

In 1867 and 1868, General Logan, then National Commander of the Grand Army of the Republic, issued proclamations officially setting aside May 30 as a day of mourning and commemoration. Many other sites thereafter took up the observance.

CARBONDALE
Cemetery
BIRTHPLACE of
DECORATION DAY

ROSCOE
MISSELHORN

ULYSSES S. GRANT HOME—Galena

"Hail to the Chief Who in Triumph Advances" read the banner the city of Galena strung across its Main Street in 1865 to welcome home the victorious Civil War Union General Ulysses S. Grant and his family. They were given the traditional hero's welcome, a triumphal ride about the town, and a fully-furnished home.

The plain little house they had left upon their Civil War-posting (and in which they had lived while Grant clerked in his father's leathergoods store) can still be seen, as can the store. There was a great difference between their arrival in Galena in 1860 by steamboat from St. Louis where Grant had failed at farming, auctioneering, and account collecting and that triumphant arrival five years later, when he returned as the most prominent of Galena's nine Civil War generals.

The spacious, two-story brick home given them (whether truly by the citizens-at-large or by a small group of local Republicans remains undetermined) had been built by Alexander J. Jackson, a leading citizen and former city clerk, about 1857-60. Located on a hillside not far from the Galena River, it is one of the finest Victorian houses in the city, an almost-intact relic of the Civil War days in architecture and appointments and it is furnished with the Grant's household effects.

Though Grant always after considered this his legal residence, he spent little time there and only in brief intervals: in 1867 he was appointed Secretary of War and oversaw the postwar Reconstruction from Washington, D.C.: in 1868 he was elected President (which news he received in the Galena home of his friend Elihu Washburne by telegraph. He was the first candidate to hear about his election by this method of communication). He was re-elected four years later, so he remained in Washington until early 1877. The Grants returned to Galena in late 1879 after a world tour, but in 1880 were off to Mexico and never returned to Galena. Grant was defeated for renomination for President and moved to New York to work on his Memoirs; there he died in 1885.

The house remained in the family until 1904 when his children deeded it to the city of Galena to be kept as a memorial to him. The city found it too great an undertaking (especially after the extensive damages done by a cyclone in 1911) and in 1931 deeded it to the State of Illinois. The Department of Conservation became responsible for it (as an Historic Site) in 1952 and, obtaining sufficient funds in 1955, began a full-restoration of the property. This took two years.

On the 135th anniversary of Grant's birth, April 27, 1957, a rededication ceremony was held at the house where he had seldom lived but always felt at home.

Gen. U.S. GRANT HOME
. Galena .

ROSCOE
MISSELHORN

The old Illinois Central Railroad Depot in Galena is still on the job—only these days its job is to house the Galena Information Center.

At one point in time its appearance had sounded the death knell for the riverboat traffic that had helped make Galena such a mining boom town, based on extensive lead deposits found near there. Worked from the time of the Indians (and "rediscovered" by the French around 1700), the site was called the River of Mines (LaFevre). The connotation of illness was not appreiciated by an area that wanted to attract settlers, so Galena (Latin for lead sulphide) came to be the name.

In 1807 the Federal Government took control of the area and leased mine sites; smelters were erected and barges started carrying the product down the Mississippi in 1810. The town was laid out in 1826, saw a big influx of miners and prospectors in the next couple of years, and by 1845 was producing over 80 per cent of the lead produced in the country. Some fortunes were made, but the river traffic more and more made Galena the leading center of trade in the Midwest. Steamboats came up the Mississippi and the Galena rivers to the very doorsteps of the city, delivering supplies for the mines, businesses, and homes, and were then used to ship out the lead.

The rough-built log and sod structures became brick and limestone. Business buildings sprang up along the bustling riverfront and homes ranged up and down on five levels along the bluffs (whose almost mountain-like landscape accents and enhances the 19th-century architecture that still adorns it).

Galena was peaking in 1845: and soon the lead would run out. Prospectors and miners were soon drawn off by the California Gold Rush and other strikes in the West. The Galena River silted up and made riverboat traffic more diffficult—and then the railroad arrived. From 1854 more and more of the river shipping was taken over by the railroad, and Galena changed from a mining boom town to a more subdued rural business-center. It continued to decline until the 1960's discovered its marketable picturesqueness and charm.

Its streets are a treasure of architectures—Federalist, Greek Revival, Victorian, Italianate—and are truly "Paths to History" as its Chamber of Commerce tour booklet was titled. It has often been called "the town that time forgot".

The multitude of restored sites includes (besides the Depot): the Ulysses S. Grant Historic Site (the pre-Civil War mansion presented to him on his return after the War); the Old Market House State Memorial at Market Square (built in 1845); the DeSoto House (hotel built in 1855 where Jenny Lind sang and Lincoln spoke); the Old Custom House (15 stagecoach lines radiated from here in 1875); and there are many other small private museums and private homes occasionally open for tours as well as dozens of antique shops.

And one can tour the source of it all—north of Galena is the Vinegar Hill Historic Lead Mine, the only one in Illinois open to the public and one which was a working mine until 1934.

GALENA

SAND

6/12/66   Depot - Galena, 911

ROSCOE
MISSELHORN

ILLINOIS CENTRAL TRAIN

When almost every other major railway was heading west into the sunset, the Illinois Central was conceived and designed to run north and south the length of the state and (very importantly) through the center of the state. For Illinois had been settled from its riverway edges "in", and (by the early 1830's) the center of the state still remained a more isolated and less populated region. Much of the land was unsuitable to the road-building techniques of the time and the population there was too busy with the chores of living to be able to maintain and repair the roads that were made.

Though the Illinois legislature incorporated the Central Railroad Company in 1837 and authorized construction from Cairo through LaSalle to Galena, the funds could not be found and the plan was abandoned. The company surrendered its charter in 1845.

Not until 1851 (and the grant of public lands to the state) was a new company (the Illinois Central) chartered and the building begun. To Stephen Douglas belonged the credit for pushing this through the legislature. It opened up the middle of the state. The rivers would no longer be the first, the easiest, and the most reliable for shipping goods and produce.

Building continued at such a pace that by September of 1856, and ahead of schedule, the track was completed and opened for traffic. This was a tremedous feat considering that this was the Cairo-Chicago line and that there was a branch from Centralia to Dunleith (opposite Dubuque on the Mississippi). It had a total mileage of 705.5 and was the longest in the world at that time. It was twice as long as any other railroad and was a worldwide marvel.

The railroad had tremendous effects on Illinois (and the nation). It founded whole towns (such as Centralia and Champaign) and affected others by its presence or absence. Rumors of the routing of any railroad could make or break town-plattings for years to come. It brought in new waves of immigrants and settlers who had either worked on the line or in the yards and shops—or were attracted by the new lands for sale. It built stations and terminals that ranged from the merely-utilitarian to architectural landmarks like Galena's Depot and Springfield's Union Station. It changed the calendar of transportation. There was no winter disruption by frozen rivers. Refrigerated shipments of beef and strawberries and other perishables became possible from 1868 on when the "Thunderbolt Express" supplied Chicago from the Centralia area. The railroad practically established coal mining as a major industry. It helped the Union win the Civil War—bringing Grant at Cairo the essential troops and war materials for the Vicksburg Campaign that secured the Mississippi Valley. And it practically destroyed the Mississippi as a long-distance commercial route (at least until economic and other changes took place in the 1970's). It cut the river's route of 1,700 miles from the Gulf to Dubuque to a direct-rail route of 950 miles.

The railroad could not stay the premier transportation method forever, of course, but the glory clings to the stations and lines that remain and the engines that preside in railway and transportation museums throughout the state (and country).

The
ILLINOIS CENTRAL
Panama Limited

ROSCOE
MISSELHORN

CAMEL ROCK—GARDEN OF THE GODS—Shawnee National Forest—Karber's Ridge

Camel Rock is impressive from any angle but is especially so when framed by Needle's Eye. It sits overlooking the Garden of the Gods Recreation Area in the Shawnee National Forest. Situated in Saline County near its intersection with Gallatin and Hardin counties, it is southeast of Harrisburg and south of Equality and Old Stone Face. Even among the extraordinary variety of this region, the Garden stands out.

The 200-million-year-old rock formations of weathered rock take on colors as varied as their shape and names: to accompany Camel Rock there is Camel Driver and Wife, Needle's Eye, Table Rock, Buzzard's Roost, Rose Rock, Anvil Rock, Noah's Ark (complete with Crocodile), Dinosaur, Turtle, Mushroom, Chimney Rock and Tower of Babel among the cylindrical sandstone columns that can reach a height of 150 feet—and there are dozens more.

There is a good mile of maintained pathway to Camel Rock and miles more of trail that lead past and through the other landmarks created by wind and water working on the stone exposed by the earth's uplift here so long ago.

The Garden is only one of many scenic, historic and recreational areas within the Forest that stretches in a broad arc from the Ohio to the Mississippi across this unusual land of the Shawnee Hills (the so-called "Illinois Ozarks"). This was the southernmost limit of the prehistoric ice sheets that scoured most of the rest of the state flat or gently rolling, and the difference persists not only in the readily-apparent features of the landscape, but also in the subtler points of flora and fauna distribution. Many of the species indigenous to the Southern Illinois area are not found elsewhere in the state.

Thanks to the lakes and waterways and the game and wildlife refuges both in and bordering the Shawnee, the area (especially its western half) is host to hundreds of thousands of waterfowl each year and it has become winter quarters for many of them.

There are seasonal "migrations" of people as well, for the hills and hollows are especially beautiful to see in the spring and fall when the flowering redbud and dogwood and the coloring oak and hickory, respectively, set off the constant pines.

But any time of the year that the trails are passable is a good time to pass by and view Camel Rock, sitting profiled in space, bearing its tufts of gnarled trees.

GARDEN OF THE GODS
NEAR EQUALITY, ILL
CAMEL ROCK

ROSCOE
MISSELHORN

SWISS MEMORIAL CHAPEL—Highland

The Swiss settlers of Highland were well-acquainted with the hazards of travel in the 19th century, for they had themselves crossed the Atlantic in the early 1830's, and they made periodic visits to family and friends back in the "old country". But in the spring of 1875, one such trip ended in a tragedy that stunned the little town and is remembered still in two memorials in the Highland City Cemetery.

Foremost among the party bound for Switzerland that year was the John Suppiger family. Suppiger, born in Switzerland in 1817, had come to Highland with his family in 1833 and here built and managed a prosperous general store. He was the original, unanimous choice for first mayor when Highland incorporated as a village in 1865, but he declined the office. Suppiger was apparently not eager to make the trip, but acceded to the wishes of his wife Catharina who wished to introduce her son-in-law-to-be to the family remaining in Switzerland. The two sailed with their 20-year-old daughter Adeline, her fiance, and their son John' (not-yet-seven).

They sailed from New York on the new German steamship "Schiller". Somewhere southwest of England they ran into bad weather, high seas, and fog. At 10 p.m., May 7, while rounding the Scilly Islands, some 20 miles off Cornwall, they struck a rock. The ship listed badly and many were washed overboard. Of the 400-some people aboard, only 44 (15 passengers; 29 crew) were saved. All of the Highland people perished.

Controversy still surrounds the sinking: a known hazardous area, a lighthouse and warning bell should have been seen or heard from the site, yet survivors said neither was. The ship fired cannon and rocket flares that went unnoticed by people nearby. In the novel *Jamica Inn,* Daphne du Maurier wrote about the Scilly Island human scavengers, who were known to turn off the light in the lighthouse and to muffle the warning bell in order that ships would wreck. The law of the sea said any wreckage of any ship belonged to whoever found it. The percentage of wrecks at this spot in Cornwall was very high. And there were seldom any survivors.

The people of Highland received word of the tragedy by telegraph the next day, and memorial services were held. A few years later they erected, with due ceremony, the first of the memorials to the loss of this well-loved family: a tall, four-sided stone obelisk bearing the names and dates of the family on three faces and a relief of a foundering ship between the simple words "Suppiger" and "Scilly Islands" on the fourth. This monument stands atop a hill within the iron-fenced Suppiger family plot.

About halfway down the slope to the south stands the second memorial (and the one pictured here)—the Chapel.

This simple, squarish white frame building with its pillared front porch has a green roof topped by a white cupola, which bears an arrow weathervane. A large iron stove sits by an inside brick chimney and 14 wood pews (bearing their donors' names) face a wooden podium inside. Its fan-lighted front door bears a plaque briefly recounting its history: "Chapel built in 1884. Presented to City of Highland July 7, 1884 by Mayor F.B. Suppiger, according to the will of John Suppiger Family who died in the Schiller shipwreck, 1875." The Chapel was declared an Historical Landmark August 8, 1974, and was restored through the efforts of the Highland Historical Society 1975.

SWISS CHAPEL
Highland

ROSCOE
MISSELHORN

LOUIS LATZER MEMORIAL LIBRARY—Highland

The library pictured is probably one of the artistic jewels of the midwest. Presented to the little town of Highland in 1929, it was endowed with 500 books and an initial Endowment Fund of $25,000. This princely (for 1929) gift was due to the fact that Pet Milk Company originated in Highland. The gift came from the widow and six children of Louis Latzer, the founder of Pet Milk Company (and its guiding genius during the difficult formative years).

By 1971 when Mrs. Jennie Latzer Kaeser (daughter of Louis Latzer) donated a new wing to the library, the size was more than doubled. And in 1983, on October 16, the New Jennie Latzer Kaeser Children's Library (another new addition) was donated. Underscoring the Latzer emphasis on the importance of education, Jennie Latzer was a graduate of the University of Illinois, class of 1900. She went on to receive a master's degree in Bacteriology in 1901—a most unusual accomplishment for a women of that day. She, however, always discounted any uniqueness by saying, "Oh, there were others. It was nothing special." But no matter what she said, it **was special.** And so was Mrs. Jennie Latzer Kaeser a very special lady who put her over-100-years of life to use in many positive ways—of benefit to everyone.

Highland, founded by large numbers of Swiss political refugees in 1837, is generally considered to be the largest Swiss settlement in the country. It was the home of the locally famous Highland and Schott Breweries, and, in the old days, the weekend picnics held at Lindendale Park brought trainloads of St. Louisans in to enjoy themselves. Traditionally the train was met by a local man mounted on horseback. He was dressed in black and wore a black top hat. His job was to lead the parade out to Lindendale Park. With numerous stops for refreshment along the way, and many more when they reached the park, some of the visitors did not make the train to carry them back to work in St. Louis, only 30 miles away.

The Swiss who founded Highland were educated people and consequently many of the streets have names of Swiss educators. There has been a consistent history of educational excellence in both public and parochial schools and the Highland Community Schools, under Olin W. Stratton Superintendent, received national and international prominence in the late 1970's.

It is said that more books have been written about Highland than about any town of its size in the country. If this is so, it is well deserved as there are a wealth of things to see and do in Highland such as: (1) a visit to the restored Latzer Homestead, (2) a look at the Bosshard Monument erected in 1909 by the Swiss Society of America, (3) a visit to the Dr. Albert Kaeser Museum and Park (for area historical items):and for fun—a visit to the Kirchenfest always held on the last Saturday and Sunday in August.

Highland receives many out-of-town visitors yearly because of its unique Swiss heritage and many of them stop by the **Swiss Villiage Book Store** which is located on Main Street in an old Swiss bank directly across from the Swiss bandstand. The **Swiss Village Book Store** was started in 1978 by Elaine Stratton, a former teacher-librarian-writer. **Swiss Village Book Store** is the publisher of this book.

LOUIS LATZER MEMORIAL
PUBLIC LIBRARY
Highland

ROSCOE
MISSELHORN

FORT DeCHARTRES—south of East St. Louis

Fort Chartres was a massive fortress and has been cited as the best constructed Fort in America. It served as the center of French power throughout the Mississippi Valley. Situated on the river about 25 miles south of St. Louis, it was the only protected place in the midwest large enough to house all men and equipment necessary to build the trading post and village that Pierre Laclede and his stepson Auguste Chouteau set up at St. Louis in 1763-64.

Begun in 1720 as a log fort, Ft. Chartres was rebuilt in 1753 in stone. The gray stone walls were fifteen to twenty feet high, three feet thick and four hundred ninety feet long. They surrounded several buildings of limestone and timber and allowed for strongly defended front and rear gates. A moat partially surrounded the fort.

In 1753, when the fort was being rebuilt in stone, the Mississippi was one and one half miles away. Ten years later the river was about 26 yards away.

In 1765 British arrived from Fort Pitt to take over from the French. They occupied the fort and renamed it Fort Cavendish and it became the seat of British government in the Illinois country until it was abandoned in 1772 and destroyed.

In 1913 the Fort Chartres (Fort Cavendish) site was acquired as a state park. The guardhouse and gatehouse have been reconstructed on the site.

Ft.
Chartres Gateway
RANDOLPH CO. ILLINOIS

ROSCOE
MISSELHORN

CAHOKIA COURTHOUSE—Cahokia

Known as the Cahokia Courthouse and as the Jean Baptiste Saucier House, this is not only the oldest courthouse in the Midwest but also the oldest surviving building in Illinois and probably the entire Midwest.

Cahokia itself is the oldest settlement in the American interior and the first permanent one in Illinois, dating from the 1699 mission established here at the summer camp of the Tamaroa Indians by three priests from the Seminary of Foreign missions. Led by the legendary French explorer Tonti, whom the Indians called "Iron Hand" from the metal hook he bore in place of one, their mission spawned a trading village already well-established by 1736/37 (when this house was built as a residence).

In 1763 Captain Saucier, a French military engineer, who had designed and built Fort de Chartres, and had resigned from the French colonial army after the Illinois country was ceded to England following the French-Indian Wars, bought the house and came with his wife to live here. In 1793 their son Francois sold the house to the American territorial government for a courthouse and jail for St. Clair County. Cahokia was the county seat when Illinois was part of the Northwest Territory and St. Clair County extended as far north as the future Chicago.

Here were held the first American court sessions in the Illinois country, part of the first election, and the region's first public school sessions.

When, because of the constant threat of floods, the county seat was moved to Belleville in 1814, the house was sold at public auction. It changed hands many times through the 19th-century and served at various times as a residence, storehouse, tavern and meeting hall.

The Courthouse appeared at the 1904 World's Fair in St. Louis and in Jackson Park, Chicago, before it returned to rest on its original foundations in Cahokia. Those restoring it in the 1930's found it originally had interior walls of plaster on split lath, casements with glass panes, shutters, beautiful wrought iron hardware, beaded beams, and ingenious roof trusses. It was comprised of four rooms and an attic with a chimney on each end. It remains a very popular tourist attraction as it approaches its 300th birthday.

ROSCOE
MISSELHORN
Apr 11 '45

CAHOKIA COURT HOUSE
CAHOKIA, ILL
BUILT BEFORE 1793.

CHURCH OF THE HOLY FAMILY—Cahokia

1949 marked the 250th anniversary of the founding of Cahokia and the Parish in which the Church of the Holy Family is located. This is the oldest church in the midwest. Its roots go back to the founding of Cahokia in 1699.

Three priests from the Seminary for Foreign Missions built a chapel and house in Cahokia. These grew into a trading village which would remain distinctly French despite British and United States rule. Since the Jesuits had previously conducted all missionary work in the region, a resounding dispute over authority arose. By royal decree from France, Cahokia was given to the Seminary and the rest of the Mississippi Valley to the Jesuits.

This church (together with the Cahokia Courthouse) is an excellent example of the colonial wood-palisade construction the French used so much throughout the Mississippi Valley in the 18th century. Called *porteaux sur sole* (post on sill), the upright logs rest on a stone foundation. Logs were of handhewn native black walnut and white oak. This church replaced an earlier structure.

Originally a simple rectangular structure 32 feet wide by 74 feet deep, it had two small wings added to its east and west sides in 1833, giving it the present cruciform shape. When a new stone church was built adjacent to it in 1891, the older building became the parish school and hall. Restoration was begun in 1949 as part of the 250th Anniversary of the founding of Cahokia and the Parish, and it was named a National Historic Landmark in 1970.

MISSION OF THE HOLY CHURCH
1787 - Cahokia, ILL

ROSCOE
MISSELHORN

ELIJAH P. LOVEJOY MONUMENT—Alton

In Alton City Cemetery stands a slim granite shaft, 93 feet high, supporting a 17-foot bronze figure of Victory and flanked by two shorter columns, each bearing an eagle with outstretched wings. It was erected in 1896 to commemorate the death, almost 60 years earlier, of Elijah Parish Lovejoy, a martyr to the cause of a free press and the abolitionist movement.

Lovejoy, originally from Maine, had emigrated to Missouri where he taught and wrote for a St. Louis newspaper. In the early 1830's he became a Presbyterian minister and became editor of the *St. Louis Observer*, a Presbyterian newspaper. He was a crusader against intemperance of all kinds and was opposed to slavery as an evil but was not then an abolitionist. With time and court actions that seemed unduly favorable to slavery, however, he became more and more outspoken in his criticism of slavery. His increasingly-strong editorials aroused such opposition and threats of violence as to prompt the moving of his press across the river to Alton.

He met strong opposition there also and his first press was broken to pieces and thrown into the river during the night of its arrival. Two other presses were destroyed during the next year as he tried to publish his *Alton Observer*. When a fourth press was ordered, a public meeting of opposition was held. At this meeting Lovejoy appeared, defending his position and the right of the freedom of the press. The press arrived five days later, November 7, 1837, and was put in a riverside warehouse where the local militia met that night.

Several of the men, including Lovejoy himself and a part-owner of the warehouse, remained as guards after the militia meeting. An armed and threatening group gathered outside and would not disperse. Shots were exchanged and one of the mob was killed. The mob increased and attempted to burn the building, but the defenders foiled the first attempt. When a second attempt was made, Lovejoy and others came out to extinguish the flames and were fired upon. Lovejoy was killed and two others wounded. The rest of the defenders agreed to a truce and free departure with a few remaining to care for the wounded and watch over Lovejoy's body. A passer-by put out the fire. The press was thrown out of the warehouse into the river.

No inquest was held, and though indictments were returned against both members of the mob and the warehouse guards, no one was ever convicted in the attack and death. But the death shocked the nation, polarizing opinion and hardening feelings on both sides of the issues and giving an immense impetus to the abolitionist movement.

Lovejoy was buried the day after his death, his 35th birthday, in a sparsely-attended funeral. His original gravesite, marked by two oaken boards, was on the bluff where the city cemetery would stand. When, a few years later, a roadway was laid out across the site, stones were lowered where the boards had been. Some time later Major Charles W. Hunter had a second grave dug and the body moved to its present location.

LOVEJOY MONUMENT
ALTON, ILLINOIS

ROSCOE
MISSELHORN

ALTON LOCKS AND DAM 26-Alton

For over 150 years the United States has been trying to "improve" the Mississippi (and Ohio) for river traffic—the new Alton Lock(s) and Dam 26 is its latest attempt.

Pictured is the "old" Alton Locks and Dam 26: the largest and costliest of the 26 sites built in the 1930's to create a nine-foot waterway in the Mississippi and to restore commercial use of the river. Originally slated for Grafton, engineers shifted it to Alton because a desirable base of operations was available in Riverside Park there and the railroad facilities were better.

Improvements to the river had been planned and attempted for a century before that time. When the Ohio and Mississippi were inspected about 1820-22, the navigable channel here had a natural depth of only 3½-4 feet at low water. Snagging, dikes and dredging were all used through the 1800's and, though some sort of permanent works was recommended in 1881, it wasn't really considered until 1910. Finally, with the River and Harbor Act of 1930, a concerted effort was made to maintain a nine-foot low-water level.

Borings made at the site found no rock to a depth of 80 feet, so it was the largest dam in the world (at least in its time) to rest entirely on a pile foundation. It was finally completed and fully opened in 1938. But the years and the river took their toll, and by the mid-60's the Corps of Army Engineers was recommending its replacement. The project began, was halted in 1974 by concerns of environmentalists and the railroads, and was resumed in 1979. It is estimated that it will take ten years to complete all three phases of the project, which is being constructed in the middle of the Mississippi two miles below Alton.

The first phase was completed by the end of 1984. In it the first of three cofferdams was built (enclosing 25 acres) and also built was the section of the dam from the Missouri shore to about halfway into the river (the lock-location). A new navigation channel was dredged, the Illinois shore was reinforced, and scenic outlooks were constructed on both sides of the river.

Phase two includes the construction of the lock itself and the building of the second cofferdam after the removal of the first. This construction will reduce the shipping channel to about 400 feet along the Illinois shore and will take about 3½ years, its estimated completion date being September 1987. The new lock is planned to be 110 feet wide and 1,200 feet long, compared with the present two that are 600 feet and 360 feet long. The present locks are unable to handle the much longer tows used on the river today without dividing them and running them through in sections. This delays traffic.

Phase three will be the construction of the dam section from the lock to the Illinois shore, the development of federally-funded recreation sites in Missouri (a first for Corps projects on this river), and perhaps the building of a hydroelectric plant. The entire project is scheduled for completion in the fall of 1989.

When the new lock is operable, alterations will be made at the old site: parts of the old dam and locks will be removed for a freer flow of traffic and the Lewis railroad bridge will have a new lift span in place of its current pivot system.

Everything about Alton Lock(s) and Dam 26 is planned to change except its number.

ALTON LOCKS

ROSCOE
MISSELHORN

RELIGIOUS CENTER (BUCKMINSTER FULLER DESIGN)—Southern Illinois University—Edwardsville

The Religious Center on the campus of Southern Illinois University at Edwardsville was built in 1971 and designed by R. Buckminster Fuller, then a visiting professor at SIUE and a world-famous architect, planner, designer, mathematician, theorist and general thinker.

Its focal point is a translucent plexiglas geodesic dome, 40 feet in circumference and 37 feet from base to top, that has been conceived and executed as a miniature earth with certain very essential properties. From inside the structure looking out toward the sky, one is literally "centered" in the earth, and Edwardsville is perceived as the center of the earth. Land and water masses (outlined and transparent blue, respectively) are figured as they would appear from that theoretical point within the true earth. And the building is so sited, bisected by the 90th meridian and so aligned that the axis of the real earth is exactly parallel to the miniature earth of the dome, thereby giving an almost-holographic view of the night skies. Fuller's plan was that stars seen at any location on the dome's face would, at that moment, be exactly in zenith over that point on the real earth.

The Dome Room is a multi-purpose area with no permanent furniture to interfere with its varying uses: theatre-in-the-round, speakers, musical groups, weddings and memorials and the regularly-scheduled worship services coordinated by the United Campus Ministry of representatives from different church bodies. It is a room of **absolute stillness.**

The Religious Center also has three meeting rooms, named for Christian martyrs: Martin Luther King, Jr.; Dietrich Bonhoeffer; and Camilo Torres. A small library of books and periodicals on religion and philosophy is provided for study and meditation. The Buckminister Fuller Religious Center is entirely non-denominational.

RELIGIOUS CENTER
· S.I.U. ,
EDWARDSVILLE

ROSCOE
MISSELHORN

MADISON COUNTY HISTORICAL MUSEUM—Edwardsville

Once the home and office of a doctor serving this community-area, the Weir House in Edwardsville has become the home of a museum serving the entire county and beyond.

John H. Weir, who had walked from Tennessee to Boston for his medical education, came west to found his practice on the nation's frontier, bringing his wife, a few pieces of furniture, and house plans from Boston over the Cumberland Road to this frontier village.

In 1836 he built the second oldest brick house in Edwardsville, the county seat since the formation of the county in 1812. The 2½-story structure is built in an early Federal style, its walls are of solid brick of local manufacture and its beams and trusses of pegged oak. Its front presents five shuttered windows up and four down with a center inset door opening into a seven-foot wide central hall that runs the full depth of the house and provides an elegant entrance with its elliptical fan light.

There are four rooms down and four up, each of them with a fireplace. The original kitchen was detached (and is long since pulled down) and a deep veranda ran across the back (west).

The doctor's office was located on the north side and had its own entrance for the convenience of family and patients. Here he served his patients and wrote articles for the medical journals of the day. From his house he went to serve as physician for the Federal prison at Alton when Confederate prisoners were housed there. He was also President of the Madison County Medical Society and practiced for 43 years before his death in 1878 at age 69.

In 1963 the house was sold to the Madison County Historical Society for a sorely-needed museum. The Society had for years worked out of limited quarters in the County Courthouse, trying to house, collate, preserve, and make available items from their collection. The Weir House now provides room for display in a setting with its own historical contribution and a bit more room for all the chores involved in museum work. They have extensive collections of items from every period of the county's history and they still mount displays in the courthouse.

It is significant that one of the rooms on the first floor of the Weir House is called the Lovejoy Room and contains Elijah P. Lovejoy's piano, for Dr. Weir, a staunch Whig, became an avid abolitionist after Lovejoy's death at the hands of the pro-slavery mob in Alton.

MADISON COUNTY
HISTORICAL MUSEUM
715 N. MAIN
EDWARDSVILLE, ILL.

ROSCOE
MISSELHORN

ST. CLAIR COUNTY COURTHOUSE (1861-1972)—Belleville

Four St. Clair courthouses have come and gone since Belleville replaced Cahokia as the county seat in 1814. The one pictured is the fourth and most lasting. It served from 1861 to 1972 when it was replaced by a more modern facility. It was classic Greek Revival architecture and was built for $108,000. In its early days it was regarded as one of the most outstanding buildings in Southern Illinois.

St. Clair County was named for Arthur St. Clair, who organized the government for the Northwest Territory and the judiciary for St. Clair County. The first court had been held at Cahokia until 1793 and Cahokia had remained the county seat until 1814. Main Street in Belleville was originally named St. Clair Street.

George Blair at one time owned almost all the property on which the original city of Belleville was built. When the decision was made (in 1814) to move the county seat to Belleville, he donated one acre of his ground to be used as a Public Square. He also donated the surrounding 25 acres for a town site. The area was at that time known as Compton Hill, and it was at his suggestion that the name was changed to Belleville (French for "Beautiful Village"). Blair's home (near the present Elks Club) was used until the first courthouse was completed.

Construction costs for the first courthouse were met from the sale of lots given to the county by Blair. All of the courthouses have been erected in about the same area. When excavation was being done for the present fifth courthouse, large underground aging and storage caves were found about ten feet under the area where the old county jail driveway had been located. The caves were said to have belonged to the old Anderson Brewery which had been located in the area.

Belleville celebrated statehood in 1818 by sinking a well on the Square and by officially becoming a town with Daniel Murray as its first president. And so the "beautiful village" headed confidently into the future. And each succeeding courthouse has re-established this optimism.

ST. CLAIR CO.
Courthouse
BELLEVILLE, ILL

ROSCOE
MISSELHORN

TINKER SWISS CHALET—Rockford

A little bit of Switzerland, that holds a little bit of almost everywhere else in the world as well, stands on the limestone bluff of Kent Creek near its junction with the Rock River.

The spacious home was inspired by Robert H. Tinker's admiration for the architectural style and atmosphere he found (and sketched) in the chalets of Switzerland that he visited during his mid-19th-century European travels. It is filled with curious and beautiful pieces he collected throughout the rest of the world: France, China, England, Germany, Italy, Hawaii and India.

Built from 1865-9, the cottage was originally reached by a suspension bridge over Kent Creek. Among its 26 rooms is a marvelous circular library, as tall as the house, with an intricately-carved spiral staircase leading to its second floor, and patterned after Sir Walter Scott's which Tinker had seen on his travels.

Tinker was as interested in Rockford as in the exotic locales he visited. He served as mayor in 1875 and was instrumental in founding the city park system which was willed the cottage and its grounds.

ROBERT H. TINKER
HOUSE
Rockford (1870)

YESTERYEAR-FRANK LLOYD WRIGHT HOUSE—Kankakee

The Yesteryear Inn was designed by Frank Lloyd Wright in 1900 and built as a private home. It now houses a nine-room inn, restaurant and gift shop and is, of course, a great tourist attraction for the Chicago area. Set on the Kankakee River, its address is Harrison at the River. Its large verandah provides an excellent vantage point for viewing those (sometimes) lazy waters. Marvin Hammack, a next-door neighbor of Roscoe Misselhorn as they were growing up, was the person who was responsible for rescuing this house from ruin and making it into a successful inn. He continued to operate it until his death in 1984. Misselhorn was a guest at Yesteryear Inn many times when he was in the Chicago area.

Yesteryear Inn is a magnificent example of Frank Lloyd Wright's "prairie style". The Inn seems a natural outgrowth of its environment. Flowing along "with" the lines of the land rather than in conflict with or in domination of it, it evokes a restful attitude well-fitting its present use.

Wright was one of the giants of American and world architecture and, as such, occupies a special place in Illinois and vice versa. From 1888 to 1893 he worked under Louis Sullivan in the offices of Adler and Sullivan in Chicago, taking over much of their residential work. In independent practice from 1893, he was experimenting with the style (he would later mature) well before the turn of the century.

Oak Park, where he lived and worked for over 20 years, is practically a gallery-display of his style, with over two dozen buildings of his design (including his house and studio built in 1891). A landmark in the evolution of modern architecture, this late-19th-century house pointed the way to 20th-century design concepts and realities. Here was his earliest attempt to merge a house into its landscape, to design it "for living". Long before the middle of the 20th-century, his "prairie style" house would be accepted in residential design. Examples of his work in houses, churches, and businesses, are found throughout this state. Though most of his later, "mature" works (residential and commercial) were done in other states and other countries, Illinois was his earliest workshop and the experience out of which he would draw the works of his lifetime.

Marvin Hammack's
"Yesteryear"
FRANK LLOYD WRIGHT
HOUSE and Gardens
KANKAKEE

ROSCOE
MISSELHORN

DAVID DAVIS HOUSE — Bloomington

Judge David Davis was a great friend and supporter of Abraham Lincoln. He and Lincoln rode together on the 8th Circuit and they made a striking pair as Davis was 6 ft. tall and weighed 300 lbs. He has often been called "The man who made Lincoln President." At the request of the Lincoln family, David Davis also administered the estate of his martyred friend. The mansion pictured here was called "Cloverlawn" and was the later-life residence of Judge David Davis.

Davis had come to Bloomington in 1836 as a lawyer and in 1848 was elected judge of Illinois' 8th Judicial Circuit, serving there until 1862 and becoming an intimate friend of Abraham Lincoln during that time. He also became one of his most potent political allies. Davis, Jesse Fell and Leonard Swett, all of Bloomington, are known as the "three musketeers" in Illinois history: the three men who groomed Lincoln for the presidency and who saw their chance at the 1860 Republican Convention to get him nominated on the third ballot.

When President, Lincoln appointed Davis to be an associate justice of the U.S. Supreme Court and he served there 15 years, afterward being elected to the U.S. Senate from Illinois.

The Davis house, set back on a landscaped lawn and surrounded by big old shade trees, was completed in 1872 and displays the ornate and substantial architectural taste of the post-Civil War era. A fine example of pure late-Victorian architecture, it boasts a mansard tower with dormers and cast-iron cresting. Built of hard-burned face brick, the walls of the restored mansion are 22 inches thick. Its fifteen rooms are graced with eight Italian marble fireplaces and furnished with period pieces that are, for the most part, original. Exhibits detail Davis's career from the days he and Lincoln rode together on the 8th Circuit.

DAVID DAVIS
HOUSE
Bloomington

ROSCOE
MISSELHORN

MORMON TEMPLE—Nauvoo

According to Mormon records, this beautiful Temple was built in accordance with a vision which appeared to their famous leader Joseph Smith. The Temple had a total life of seven years from the time it was started in 1841, dedicated in 1846, and fired by arsonists in 1848.

The Mormons had fled from Missouri because of religious persecution. When they settled in the area around Nauvoo, they thought they were safe. Nauvoo was incorporated in 1841 with a special charter from the state legislature granting it complete home rule save for violations of state and/or federal constitution. The population reached a peak of about 20,000 before conflicts between Mormons and other settlers in the area culminated in the 1844 killings of Joseph Smith and his brother Hyrum while they were being held in the Carthage jail (plural marriage was the cause).

The Mormons in Nauvoo left Illinois to go west—they ended their trek in Salt Lake City. The two custodians who were left behind to guard the Temple were unable to prevent its destruction.

The Temple sat on the crest of a hill facing west. A broad stairway of ten steps led up to three arched doorways and into the foyer. Circular stairways gave access to the other levels. The baptistry had a font of white limestone resting on the backs of twelve white oxen. The tower held a belfry with the Temple bell (removed to Utah in 1846), an observatory topped with a cupola, and a spire topped by a weathervane of a flying angel. The building design combined elements of various architectural styles from classical to the nineteenth century. Walls were of native gray limestone from nearby quarries (with blocks four to six feet thick). In size the Temple extended 128 feet east and west, 88 feet north and south and it reached 60 feet from ground to eaves. The tower and spire rose another 98 feet. There were moonstones at the base of the pilasters, sunstones as capstones and star stones decorating the frieze. There were 30 of each of these adorning the 30 pilasters that ranged around the building. They were all hand-tooled and polished on the site from limestone blocks.

Only the walls were left standing after arsonists fired the building in 1848. These walls, however, were used by another visionary sect of Utopian believers, as Etienne Cabot and his French Icarians settled in and practiced their communal life before disbanding—leaving behind them a thriving wine-making industry continued by the German immigrants who followed.

A cyclone in 1850 blew down the north wall and so weakened the south and east walls that they had to be razed. The front of the building survived to about 1865. The site was thereafter used as a quarry, with its stone used in local buildings and even barged off-site (to Galena and Dubuque).

Recent excavations have revealed the original foundations of the Temple. The moonstones are fairly plentiful. Only one starstone was recovered and only three sunstones—one is in the Smithsonian, one at the Quincy Historical Society Museum, and one remains at Nauvoo in the fenced enclosure in the State Park area to watch over the remains and reconstruction of its famous site.

The TEMPLE of NAUVOO

ROSCOE MISSELHORN

JAMES MILLIKIN HOUSE—Decatur

This imposing brick Victorian mansion, home of James & Anna Millikin, was considered one of the most impressive homes in this area of the state when it was completed in 1876 at a cost of $18,000. It now houses the Decatur Art Institute as provided in the will of Anna Millikin in 1913.

The 2½-story house of red brick has tall, narrow windows with white-stone caps; tall, spacious verandas with the fanciful wood trim of the period; wide stone steps; lead glass; a low-pitched mansard roof; and, dominating the front, a mansarded cupola with bull's eye windows and an ornate cast-iron cresting.

Millikin University in Decatur was established in 1901 by James Millikin who was sympathetic to the struggles of students to acquire an education. As a former herdsman (drover) he had driven a herd of steers from Pennsylvania to New York driving them right down Broadway. He studied at Washington College, Pennsylvania, and then resumed droving. This time he drove a flock of sheep to Illinois, liked the country and stayed. He has been called the "First Cattle King of the Prairie State" and he became a very wealthy man.

In 1856 he came to Decatur and became involved in real estate and banking. He established the Millikin National Bank in downtown Decatur in 1860. But the crowning point in his life was the establishment of Millikin University. He was able to oversee the first 8 years of its life before he died in 1909.

The University & Art Institute remain as his legacy to Decatur.

JAMES MILLIKIN
HOUSE
Decatur

ROSCOE
MISSELHORN

CARL SANDBURG BIRTHPLACE—Galesburg

From a simple workman's cottage, like millions of others throughout the nation, came one of America's greatest poets. In this one-story frame house without even a porch or stoop (one steps in from a rectangular flagstone) Carl Sandburg was born and spent his earliest childhood.

The house is only a stone's throw from the Galesburg railroad shops where Carl Sandburg's father worked a forge for the Burlington line. Sandburg's father was a Swedish immigrant who changed his name to Sandburg from its original Johnson, (reportedly after a pay mix-up among the innumerable "Johnsons" working in the shops).

As the family fortunes improved, they bought a house similar to the one they rented, and still later moved to larger and more comfortable quarters.

As Sandburg's national and international fame grew, attention was refocused on that little workman's cottage where he had been born. Thanks largely to the efforts of Mrs. Adda George of Galesburg, the site was purchased and restored by the Carl Sandburg Association (which she organized) and opened to the public as a dual, Sandburg-Lincoln museum. The site is now a State Memorial and contains various memorabilia of both men including Sandburg's autographed works and the typewriter on which he wrote his masterful biography of his fellow Illinoisan and man of the people.

There is a Remembrance Rock in the park next door, and the poet's ashes are buried behind the house.

MISSELHORN BARN

Roscoe Misselhorn is famous for his covered bridges, trains, riverboats and barns. The barn in this drawing (done in his 83rd year) is one of his best. Located in Randolph County, it typifies the hundreds of barns he has drawn.

It was land that drew the settlers to the Illinois country, and Illinois has made substantial contributions in agriculture ever since. First settled were the fertile bottom lands which were most accessible because they were along the riverways into the country. They were first-settled, but they were hazardous with their periodic flooding. Flooding led the people on to the less-fertile uplands that developed so well into dairy operations with beef cattle and other livestock; or to the lands that adapted to orchards. From Cobden in 1866 came the first refrigerated rail-shipment of fruit in the United States.

Then there was the long holdout—the prairie. The prairie was last settled because there was a lot of space but there were no trees (or not many) for all the essentials of fuel and buildings and fences. The ground was rich, but it was so thick and clinging that the farmers spent more time cleaning their plows than plowing. Prairie fires were also a constant danger. But still, so tempting was it that settlers worked bit by bit, until Illinois gave them the tool that would "take the prairie"—the self-cleaning steel plow John Deere invented and made in Grand Detour in the 1830s.

The 1830-40s saw an agricultural revolution: it seemed men were inventing all kinds of horse-drawn machinery: reapers, threshers, cultivators, etc. All of it was gloriously displayed at the first Illinois State Fair and at state and county fairs ever after.

Agriculture was always more than "just" the farming. It was the blacksmithing and machinery-making, the repairing, the milling, the food processing, the transporting and storing, the auctioning and marketing, and the researching and testing.

J.B. Turner gave Illinois the Osage Orange, the best fence around until a couple of fellows in DeKalb invented barbed wire. Turner's push for industrial universities led to land-grant colleges and the University of Illinois, the Morrow Plots, and hybrid seeds.

Most farms became mechanized from World War I on; by the 1920's the automobile brought the need for good hard roads that made trucking crops easier, too. Before that there had been trouble between the railroads and farmers—having to do with rate and fare charges—until Illinois (in the 1870s) established the legal precedent of regulation in the public interest.

It was the wealth and security of the land (as penned in the stockyards and grain elevators and untouched by flames) that insured Chicago's rebuilding after the Great Fire of 1871. It was the shared richness of the milder-seasoned Southern Illinois that had also seen the state through the incredibly cold winter of 1830. Forever-after that time, Southern Illinois was called "Egypt" after the Ancient World's granary.

Illinois has seen all types and styles of farming from the subsistence of early settlers, the large spreads of the early 1800s, the economically-efficient family-sized farms that worked so well for so long, and the newer business-enterprise trend.

And as that family farm remains for many people **the** farm, so the barn remains its most traditional symbol. Seen in all styles of architecture through all parts of the state, in all conditions of repair or deterioration, a barn still standing marks the site of a farm.

Retreating
Snow
LEANDERVILLE ROAD
Randolph County

ROSCOE
MISSELHORN

Dec 27 '89

JOHN DEERE HISTORIC SITE—Grand Detour

Here at Grand Detour, so named by early French traders from the horseshoe bend in the Rock River where it stands, the face of American (or at least Midwestern) farming was changed and the fate of the prairie sealed. For here, in the 1830s, John Deere fashioned a new plow from a broken Sheffield-steel sawblade and demonstrated on some of the stickiest bottom-land soil he could find that the blade did what none of the older styles had been able to do—it cut sharply through the ground and cleaned itself as it plowed.

Deere and Major Leonard Andrus, fellow-Vermonters who had founded the village just a few years before, began to manufacture the plow here, and the presence of the Deere & Andrus plow factory helped boom the town into the 1840s.

Then the railroad bypassed the village, and Deere decided to sell his interest to Major Andrus and move to Moline, where he established a larger operation that is still based there. Grand Detour settled into its comfortably picturesque 19th-century atmosphere.

The reconstructed blacksmith shop of that era includes a forge and tools such as Deere would have used in his trade. It is part of the John Deere Historic Site in the center of the town, which also includes Deere's home (re-purchased by a granddaughter many years after the family had moved) and authentically furnished, and a building housing the exact site of the original blacksmith shop that changed the history of the American Frontier.

122

JOHN DEERE
Historic Site
GRAND DETOUR

ROSCOE
MISSELHORN

SILKWOOD MANSION (HALFWAY HOUSE)—Mulkeytown

Silkwood Mansion (or Halfway House) in Mulkeytown is best viewed in the summer, for it is then that a small, red-flowered hollyhock (of a type not usually seen in the North) blooms and brings back memories of the "Quadroon Girl" who first planted them here.

In the 1820s Basil Silkwood built this log house (clapboard-covered since the late 1800s) beside the Shawneetown-Kaskaskia Trail. It was about a half-mile north of Mulkeytown and about halfway along the Trail. Silkwood kept a tavern in part of the building and he and his wife lived in the rest of the house. Though childless, they foster-parented some sixteen orphans over the years—one of them was the "Quadroon Girl" named Priscilla.

Priscilla had started life as a slave on the Carolina (or Georgia) plantation of a friend of Silkwood's. He had visited this friend in the early 1830s and there he first met Priscilla. Upon the death of their master (shortly thereafter), the slaves were sold at auction with the rest of his property. Priscilla was bought by a Cherokee Indian chief and taken to the Great Smoky Mountain region in western Carolina.

In 1838 came the government decree that the Cherokee must move west of the Mississippi River to resettlement in the Indian Territory. A hard-working and prosperous people, they were forbidden to take much of their property with them, though they were allowed to keep some slaves. So Priscilla started out with her Indian master on what would later be known as the "Trail of Tears". They were camped for part of the winter near Jonesboro, close to the spring crossing-point at Cape Girardeau, when Silkwood (on a business trip to the town) saw and recognized Priscilla. He bought her from her Indian master and she returned with him to the house at Mulkeytown. Though freed, she remained with the family there until her death in 1892. Her grave, marked by a shapeless sandstone, is beside the graves of the Silkwood family in Reed Cemetery north of the house.

But a more vivid reminder of Priscilla returns each summer for, from her first home on that plantation so far to the east where they had bloomed so beautifully, she had brought the hollyhocks she had loved as a child. She had carried the seeds to her new home in the Great Smokies and on from there to her last home with the Silkwoods. Here they still bloom and, indeed, have now gone on to complete that last journey west Priscilla did not finish. It is said that seeds from the flowers at the Silkwood House were sent to the daughter of the last Cherokee chief in Oklahoma in the 1950s.

May 21 '45

ROSCOE
MISSELHORN

Half Way House
MULKEYTOWN
The SILKWOOD HOUSE

JOHN WOOD MANSION—Quincy

It is especially fitting that John Wood's mansion today houses the Quincy and Adams County Historical Society, since he and his house were so great a part of the area history.

John Wood hailed originally from Cayuga County, New York and had come West and farmed in Pike County for several years before visiting the site of the present Quincy. He liked the location, and returned to it in 1822 when he built a log cabin. It was the first house to be built in that locality.

Wood's fortune and fame grew with the town. He served as a trustee of the village and then as mayor. In the State Senate, he was a friend and supporter of Abraham Lincoln and one of the organizers of the Republican Party. He was Lieutenant Governor in 1860 when Governor Bissell died and Wood served out the term. During the Civil War he not only served as quartermaster general of Illinois but also led the 137th Illinois Infantry into action though he was then 66 years old.

In 1835 John Wood built the pictured stately Greek Revival home on the Mississippi riverfront. Here he entertained friends and associates from throughout the state and observed Quincy's rise from a village of log and frame houses to its eminence as a riverport.

The pillared, two-story house now contains mementos of Governor Wood and his family. (Such mementos as his Civil War pistols, and the sword and medical books his surgeon-father carried in the Revolutionary War.) It also contains mementos of Quincy and Adams County and many other items of historical interest. The seventeen rooms of the mansion are fitted with fine furnishings of the period including a lovely chandelier of French-drop crystals that once glistened in the salon of a Mississippi River Steamboat.

Quincy's most historic dwelling is on the National Register of Historic and Landmark Buildings.

126

JOHN WOOD MANSION
QUINCY

ROSCOE
MISSELHORN

WILLIAM JENNINGS BRYAN HOUSE—Salem

A political power for three decades, the power base of William Jennings Bryan was from Nebraska although he was born here in Salem, in March 1860. It was from Illinois that Bryan entered the practice of law, following the footsteps of his father, who often told his son how in 1852 he had helped hew the timbers used in the building of their home.

The Bryan family lived in the home until young William was about six years old. Then the family moved to a country home outside Salem. It was not until William Bryan was 27 years old that he moved to Lincoln, Nebraska and became interested in politics.

The house in Salem is small and white-painted with a small porch across the front. A small entry hall runs back through the center of the house with the sitting room on one side and the parlor on the other: these are now museum rooms with Bryan memorabilia. There is a kitchen and dining room at the rear on the first floor and two bedrooms on the second floor. Adjoining is the Bryan-Bennett Library, a newer building of simple but distinguished architecture, which Bryan himself dedicated in 1908.

William Jennings Bryan was known as the "silver tongued" orator, and he was a staunch advocate of free silver as opposed to the gold standard (dollar backed by gold). He almost defeated Grover Cleveland on this issue and the "Cross of Gold" speech he delivered at the Democratic convention of 1896 brought him more votes than were received by Cleveland—who was the winner.

The Scopes Trial, in which a schoolteacher John T. Scopes was convicted for teaching Darwin's evolutionary theory, brought greatest fame to Bryan as he served as prosecution attorney. He won his case, although Clarence Darrow's defense proved devastating. Bryan died less than a week after the trial ended on July 26, 1925.

William Jennings

ROSCOE MISSELHORN

BJORKLUND HOTEL—Bishop Hill

Bishop Hill was the site of a prairie utopia founded in 1846 by Swedish immigrants and named after their leader Eric (Erik) Janson. Of the many utopian communities which sprang up on the prairies, this could be considered one of the more successful; although it, like all the others, ultimately failed.

The religious dissenters came by way of the Erie Canal and the Great Lakes to Illinois and settled, literally "digging in" their first winter: hollowing out caves in a gorge near South Edwards Creek. The following spring they began to establish their religious, communistic colony which in 15 years went from underground shelters and log cabins to nearly 20 buildings of home-made bricks. The settlement of highly-skilled farmers and artisans became the most important settlement between Rock Island and Peoria.

Two principal crops were broomcorn and flax. Broomcorn was harvested, dried and sorted at the colony, then taken by wagon to a Galena warehouse where it was loaded on railroad cars for shipment East; and flax, which the colonists used to make linen, also sold on the national market.

Though it prospered briefly and had at one time 1,500 members, Janson's murder in 1850 by a non-member of the colony who had been attempting to remove his colonist wife and child from the group, and the economic and religious dissension that followed in the next few years, led to its formal dissolution in 1861. The land was distributed among the adult members of the colony, whose descendants are presently restoring the site.

Twelve of the original buildings are still standing including the Bjorklund Hotel, restored though not open to overnight guests; the Steeple Building, whose bell and clock were made by the colony blacksmith and which houses the Henry County Historical Museum; and the Colony Church, the first permanent structure, erected in 1848 (and the first restored). It contains a collection of the famous prairie primitive painter Olaf (Olof) Krans, a resident of the community who was a blacksmith by trade and a self-taught artist.

The site was designated an Illinois State Memorial in 1946, an Illinois State Historic Landmark in 1969, and then a National Historic Landmark.

The beautiful, tiny hamlet of about 200 people hosts a September harvest festival: Jordbruksdagarna (Jordbruk Dagen).

July 10 66

HOTEL BISHOP HILL ILL

ROSCOE
MISSELHORN

WHITE SQUIRRELS—Olney

Olney was, for many years, known as ''the home of the white squirrels'' because (sometime between 1902 and 1906) a pair of albino squirrels were liberated in Olney by someone-possibly Dr. Robert Ridgway, a naturalist who established an arboretum (of essentially native trees) in Olney in 1906 and named it Bird Haven.

Results from the original albino pair of squirrels were astounding and at one time it was estimated that there were thousands of the little creatures scampering around. There are still some, but they have co-habited with grey squirrels so long that they are no longer so easy to find as in former years—except in advertising around town where the White Squirrel appears as a name or symbol everywhere—even on the uniforms of the police.

Dr. Robert Ridgway was a naturalist and one time curator of the division of birds at the United States National Museum in Washington, D.C. He was founder of the Ornithologists Union and he came from (and retired to) Olney where he died in 1929 and was buried in his arboretum (Bird Haven). A simple granite boulder marks his grave.

WHITE SQUIRRELS
Olney 911

R.M.

ROSCOE
MISSELHORN '45

PETERSTOWN HOUSE—Waterloo

The National Register of Historic Places accepted Peterstown House as one of its own in 1977 because it is the only intact structure still left on the Kaskaskia Frontier Trail from Fort deChartres to Cahokia. The building takes its name from an early community which eventually became the northern part of Waterloo.

Founder Emery Peter Rogers came to the area from Massachusetts in about 1830, bought a tract of land, and shortly after built a stagecoach stop. In 1858 he sold the building to Valentine Sturtzum who enlarged it. It then became known as Sturtzum's Hall and was an early social center in Waterloo. It was converted into apartments in the 1930's and later fell into disrepair. The Peterstown Heritage Society purchased it in 1970 and restored the downstairs as a country store and local history museum while the upstairs was restored as a large meeting room. The two log cabins at the rear of the property were occupied by early Monroe County families and were brought to Waterloo in 1975.

Peterstown House is a two-story saltbox-style house 49 feet wide by 40 feet deep. The southern portion rests on a limestone foundation and the northern portion rests on sandstone. Its strong foundation, and more than a little hard work and luck, have helped it endure to this day.

PETERSTOWN HOUSE
Waterloo, Ill.

ROSCOE
MISSELHORN

HALFWAY STAGE COACH HOUSE—Iuka (Salem)

This Halfway Tavern was located on the Vincennes Trace. It missed the original making of the buffalo trails and their early use by the prehistoric Indian tribes in following the herds, but it has seen every other change in land travel.

It began with the old "St. Louis Trace," possibly the first overland trail in the Illinois country, and it followed one of these even-earlier buffalo trails for much of its route. An extension of the Wilderness Road that ran from the Cumberland Gap to Vincennes, Indiana, this then continued from Vincennes and ran across Illinois to Kaskaskia, Cahokia, and St. Louis. This (the Vincennes-Kaskaskia mail route) was the earliest mail-route in Illinois, so-designated by the federal government in 1805. The Vincennes-Shawneetown route was added the next year and the mail service reached St. Louis via Prairie du Rocher and Cahokia from Kaskaskia in 1810. The mail in those days was carried by horseback, horse-drawn buggy or covered wagon until about 1819 when stagecoaches became common enough for a stageline to be established on the trail. It was the oldest interstate stagecoach route in Illinois.

By Illinois' statehood in 1818, this route ran across still-unsurveyed country, though a number of tavern keepers were locating at the approximately 20-mile intervals needed for stopovers, team changes, etc. A few other settlers had assembled at these points and, in what is now Marion County, a little settlement of ten or twelve families was located in the general Salem area.

Throughout the 1840's stagecoaches ruled Illinois roads. The fact that it was a mail route entitled this road to a higher priority in maintenance and repair (for the mails had to go through). County commissioners were authorized to open, maintain and improve public roads, of course, but there was no well-established, permanent system for that upkeep. For years to come it would depend on the donation of labor by public-spirited citizens along any given route. Roads that were little trouble in summer and the hard-frozen days of winter, turned into bogs of deep, clinging mud with spring and autumn rains; and the skill of one's driver mattered as much as the condition of the road-face. Travel was still hard and uncomfortable and the stations a welcome relief. And every route had a Halfway House or Tavern.

Salem, though incorporated in 1837, dates its founding to 1823 and the second house built there was Mark Tully's stopping place for the Vincennes stage. Iuka was a settlement near Salem so-called because Civil War veterans, who had fought in the battle of Iuka in 1862, wished to commemorate that Union victory. The Iuka Halfway Stage Coach House now stands in Salem, restored to the way it looked in 1817-18 when it was built, and it watches a new age of traffic go by.

OLD HALFWAY TAVERN
VINCENNES TO ST. LOUIS
BUILT 1818
IUKA, ILL.

ROSCOE
MISSELHORN
JULY 11 '45

OLD TIPPLE COAL MINE—Pinckneyville

Many parts of the southern part of the state once resembled a desolate war-torn battlefield. Strip-mining may have been the cheapest method of mining, but it left ruin behind. State law now requires that the environment be restored after the coal has been stripped from its close-to-the-surface beds.

It seems Illinois has always been known for its coal, for the very first mention of the bituminous variety anywhere in North America was noted in 1673 by Joliet and Marquette in the Ottawa-Utica area. (They called it "Charbon de terre.") While some of the early rail shipments came from this region, the main beds lay further south and that is where the commercial mining began near Murphysboro along the Big Muddy River in 1810. Murphysboro coal smelted Missouri iron ore at Grand Tower furnaces until the 1870s (indeed, Andrew Carnegie for a time considered this area for a "Pittsburgh of the West").

Drift or slope mines were used at first to work exposed seams on bluffs or hillsides and the coal was shipped on the rivers that were the main transportation routes. In the 1840s some coal was being shipped in wagons on roads. Then came the railroads. they burned coal (the first wood-to-coal-burning engine conversion came from Centralia's Illinois Central shops). Coal was also needed to produce steel for rails and the industrial revolution increased fuel needs. The real push for Illinois coal development was on.

Illinois, this country's first bituminous coal site, still has one of the largest reserves of that type of coal. Unfortunately, it is not of the high grade required to meet present environmental standards.

Coal has long been a touchy barometer of the economy: it has founded towns (like Ziegler) in good times and "ghosted" them in bad (or when the coal itself gave out). It drew workers from as far away as Wales and eastern Europe and could as easily cast them adrift.

Mining has been hazardous, hard and uncertain, and miners have been at the forefront of labor organizing from the beginning. Memorials to those lost in mine accidents or strike actions dot the state.

And memorials to the coal and its mining remain: like an old tipple standing here at Pinckneyville (where shovels now strip but the reclamation continues). Or some other structure or spur line of a railroad indicating where an old slope or shaft mine once was. Or a slag heap on the landscape like a headstone marking the site not of a burial, but rather of a removal from the earth of Illinois. And amid the memorials—some working mines continue.

OLD TIPPLE
PINCKNEYVILLE

ROSCOE
MISSELHORN

SUSPENSION BRIDGE—Carlyle

Spanning the Kaskaskia River on the east side of Carlyle is the only bridge of its kind in Illinois. Originally called the Carlyle Suspension Bridge, it was renamed in 1953 in honor of Major General William F. Dean, a native of Carlyle, who was awarded the Congressional Medal of Honor for heroism as a P.O.W. in the Korean Conflict.

The bridge, begun in 1859 by Griffith D. Smith, a Pennsylvania contractor, cost $45,000 and provided a permanent crossing on the Kaskaskia for traffic on the Goshen Road and the St. Louis Trace. The 180-foot, single-span frame structure had a ten-foot wide bridge deck supported by two parallel wire rope cables suspended between four 35-foot stone towers with gravity anchors at both approaches.

It was heavily used until the 1920's; then a steel truss bridge was built 300 feet downstream to accomodate U.S. Route 50 traffic. In 1946 the Carlyle Suspension Bridge Restoration Association was formed to save the abandoned and badly-deteriorated structure. When the Historic American Building Survey cited it for architectural significance and recommended its preservation in 1950, the State appropriated funds toward the restoration. In 1952 it was restored as a 6-foot-wide pedestrian crossing of the Kaskaskia and so it remains. It was listed on the National Register of Historic Places in 1973.

Near this swinging footbridge is Illinois' largest man-made lake, the 26,000-acre Carlyle Lake. This lake, which extends into four Southern Illinois counties (Bond, Clinton, Fayette and Marion), was formed from damming the Kaskaskia River, the river itself being rechannelled to flow through a concrete spillway. Carlyle Lake is well known by sailing and fishing enthusiasts of the St. Louis area. Eldon Hazlett and South Shore State Parks adjoin Lake Carlyle and furnish additional camping and recreation areas.

SUSPENSION BRIDGE
CARLYLE

R. MISSELHORN   APH 16 58

MINERAL SPRINGS HOTEL AND BATH HOUSE—Okawville

During the 19th century (1800's) there were a number of mineral water spas all over the country. In that day what was the fashion in Europe was the fashion here, and (in Europe) mineral baths were the fashion. The old Mineral Springs Hotel in Okawville is the last remaining one of its sort still in operation in Illinois. It is located at 301 East Walnut St. and is listed on the National Register of Historic Sites.

Okawville was laid out as a town in 1856. Prior to that time, the tiny settlement was called Bridgeport. In 1867, when digging a well, Okawville businessman Rudolph Plegge found an unusual kind of water—it bubbled. For advice, Plegge contacted a friend (C.H. Kelle) who had worked at the famous bath center at Baden-Baden, Germany before coming to America. Kelle told him how such a discovery would be handled in Europe, and Plegge went into the mineral spring business.

Samples of the water were sent to St. Louis for analysis. The report was sent back indicating that the water had very strong medicinal qualities. Plegge decided that he would build a small bath house to treat rheumatism and other related diseases. Dr. McIlwain of Okawville (also an early consultant on the project) agreed to handle the medical side of the business and a small bathhouse was opened at the Spring. The Reverend J.F. Sherbaum later bought the business and erected a modern bath complex and resold it. In 1871 a large hotel replaced the small bath house and four additional hotels were opened. The original building burned in 1892 and was rebuilt. It is the one standing today.

The hotel is a two-story white frame structure which has a wooden veranda extending along the two street sides of the building. It is 162 feet wide and 38 feet deep. The bath house is a two story brick structure connected to the hotel by an elevated wooden passageway. The Bath House measures 60 feet wide by 110 feet deep. The buildings look, and are used, much as they were at the turn of the century.

Another such spa can be seen at Grantfork (originally Grant's Fork) ten miles north of Highland. This one is called Diamond Mineral Springs. It was at one time a preferred summer resort for St. Louisans who would come over to spend the summer "taking the waters," strolling, visiting, socializing, and resting (weekends they would be joined by the gentlemen of the family). Gone is the hotel and springs—remaining (and still in operation) is the large dining hall and dance hall which still looks almost exactly as it did in 1900.

At a smaller hotel in the town of Grantfork (the hotel that took the overflow from the big hotel at Diamond Mineral Springs) the story is told how one day, in the middle of the boarding house meal, there was a loud crash. Tumbling through the ceiling onto the middle of the table crashed a vagrant who had hidden himself in a closet just above the dining room and had gone to sleep. Rudely awakened, he was surprised to find himself on the table being served for dinner.

ORIGINAL SPRINGS
Okawville.

ROSCOE
MISSELHORN

APPELLATE COURT—Mt. Vernon

This beautiful building of Greek Revival design was originally built in 1854 in order to house the southern grand division of the Illinois Supreme Court. When that court was moved to Springfield in 1897, it then became headquarters of the Fourth District Appellate Court.

Clara Barton, founder of the American Red Cross, used the courthouse as a hospital following the great tornado of 1881. It was in this building, also, that Lincoln won his famous tax case for the Illinois Central Railroad in 1859.

Built of gray brick and stone in the shape of a Maltese cross, the entrance pavilion is adorned with fluted Ionic columns and it is topped with a fine classic pediment. The arched portal is approached by a long double flight of cast iron steps that lend a very graceful air to this lovely and unusual building.

APPELATE
COURT
MT. VERNON

ROSCOE
MISSELHORN
1945

BALD KNOB CROSS OF PEACE—Alto Pass

Visible from 20 miles away and especially impressive when illuminated at night, the Bald Knob Cross of Peace stands today because of the idea and efforts of a local mail carrier and a pastor.

The immediate result of a conversation between Wayman Presley and Reverend William Lyerla following rural church services in the early spring of 1937 was the first Easter sunrise service held on Bald Knob (two or three weeks later) with about 250 people present. Word of the event had been spread by Mr. Presley along his mail route and throughout the nearby countryside. As the services have continued to be held regularly since, and the roadway to the site has been improved, more and more people have come great distances to attend.

In 1951 the services were becoming so popular and involved that the Bald Knob Christian Foundation was incorporated and steps were taken to establish a permanent memorial garden or shrine on the top of the mountain. A tract of land, including 80 acres that had been bought from the United States in 1870, was deeded to the Foundation in 1953, and plans were made to gather funds and erect an appropriate structure.

The great 130-foot Cross has sprung from three crude wooden ones first erected for the services on this site. Bald Knob Mountain is one of the highest points in Southern Illinois, rising over 100 feet above sea level and commanding a view of over 600 square miles. It is a most impressive vantage point, especially when one is facing East from this slope and watching the dawn light the distant hills. Each Easter, celebrated in such a beautiful setting, has special meaning.

Wayman Presley went on to found Presley Tours and has become known world wide—all because a rural mailman had a dream.

BALD KNOB CROSS
ALTO PASS

ROSCOE
MISSELHORN

MARY'S RIVER COVERED BRIDGE—Chester

The builder of the Mary's River Covered Bridge was a professional European bridge builder from Germany. His name was Wilhelm Misselhorn and he was the grandfather of Roscoe Misselhorn, the artist of this book. This was a fact not known by his grandson when he made his first sketch of the Mary's River Covered Bridge in the 1920's.

Wilhelm Misselhorn was hired to build this bridge in 1854 because of his impressive credentials. He had an engineering diploma from Hamburg, Germany, dated July 15, 1839. It certified him as a European Bridge Building specialist. He had gained much practical experience in helping to build the bridge at Hanover, Germany. Wilhelm Misselhorn also received an additional diploma from Copenhagen on April 14, 1845, not long before he came to America. He built the Mary's River Bridge from native white oak timbers in a Burr arch design with double arches on either side of the King posts—this is somewhat the same style used by James Eads in his long standing Eads Bridge. The Mary's River structure rested on stone abutments and most of the original timber is still preserved even though the bridge was in continuous service from 1854 to 1930. It was originally part of a planned toll road between Bremen and Chester. and was privately owned by a Mr. Hartman. In the early 1870's the bridge and planked road were sold to Randolph County as part of the county road system. The state of Illinois purchased it in 1936 in order to preserve it. The bridge is 86 feet long by 18 feet wide with vertical clearance of twelve feet. It is the only bridge of its kind left in Southern Illinois.

MARYS RIVER
BRIDGE

R. MISSELHORN

MARINE WAYS NAVAL STATION—Mound City

When Cairo was a great river port, it was not unusual for 100 boats per day to use the docks. These boats required building and repairing. It was for this reason the Marine Ways was established at Mound City. Old shipyard records were destroyed by fire years ago so not a lot of information has survived. It is known, however, that iron-clad gunboats built in this shipyard played an important role in the defense of the Mississippi River and the capture of Vicksburg during the Civil War. James B. Eads (builder of the famous Eads Bridge connecting East St. Louis and St. Louis) was also in charge of building iron-clads in this important naval shipyard located ten miles north of Cairo on the Ohio River.

The shipyard was completed in 1859, built by a Cincinnati firm as part of a planned great city at the site. It was to have been called "Emporium City." The first boat serviced was the barge "Memphis" in 1859. During the Civil War the national government took over the shipyards and used it as part of the naval station at Cairo. Iron ore was needed to make the armored boats and this was supplied from a site now in the Shawnee National Forest.

Little now remains of the once great naval shipyard on the Ohio River.

MARINE WAYS
MOUND CITY, ILL.

Roscoe
Misselhorn

May 20 '45

CHARTER OAK SCHOOL—Randolph County

This unique eight-sided schoolhouse is one of the only two left in the United States. Built in the early 1870's, it was constructed as a single classroom with eight walls each about ten feet wide by thirteen feet high. It was used for over 84 years until the end of the 1953-54 school year.

The first school building on this site was a more traditional log cabin which was destroyed by a tornado in 1870. At the time the school was first built, it was named the Charter Oak School because a large oak tree was near the building and it reminded someone of the historic Charter Oak of New England.

Tradition says that Daniel Ling (an early teacher from the East) knew of an eight-sided school in Valley Forge, Pennsylvania. He convinced the school authorities that the eight sides would be more resistant to strong winds (a consideration since the first school was lost to a tornado). Another point in favor of the unusual construction was that it provided more natural lighting with a window in each of the eight sides.

Originally the teacher's desk was to be located in the center of the Charter Oak School and pupils were to sit in rows around walls with narrow aisles between sections facing the teacher's desk. Since some of the Randolph County students were inclined to let their minds wander from their lessons, it was found to be impractical to have the teacher seated with his back to some of the pupils.

The cloakroom (a necessary part of all schools) was also not included in the original building. It was added to the school as an addition in 1910 and it proved a much better place to keep lunches, hats and coats, and the occasional mischief makers who were, after all, farmers first and scholars second. This was reflected in student attendance, which fluctuated according to the seasonal demands of farming.

Charter Oak School has been used for many purposes over the years. Literary Society meetings, church services, political meetings, box socials, and farmers' organization meetings are just a few of the uses to which the school was put. Currently owned by the Randolph County Historical Society (owners since 1960), Charter Oak School has been faithfully restored to much of its original unique flavor.

Charter Oak
8 sided school
RANDOLPH CO. ILL.

ROSCOE
MISSELHORN

1776-1976

UNIVERSITY HALL—FIRST BUILDING OF UNIVERSITY OF ILLINOIS—Champaign/Urbana

Pictured is the first building (no longer standing) of the University of Illinois at Champaign-Urbana—this is a building which actually predates the school itself. It all began with plans in 1859 for a Methodist seminary to be established at West Urbana (which later would become Champaign in 1860). This, the "Urbana & Champaign Institute" building, was begun in 1861, but construction was interrupted by the Civil War and the original parties were unable to continue with their original plan. After President Lincoln signed the Morrill Act creating the land-grant universities, Champaign County offered the property (and uncompleted building) as part of its bid for the site of this Illinois university. The building, commonly called "the Elephant" (partly from its rather ungainly appearance and partly from its "white elephant" status with the local citizens) was still unfinished in 1867 when Champaign County was awarded the location of the university. It required extensive remodeling to ready it for the opening of classes of the Illinois Industrial College (as the school was chartered) the next year.

This building housed the classrooms, dorms, chapel and club rooms of the over-100 students who were in attendance. It was damaged by a wind storm in 1880 and revamped when rebuilt. Its function, of course, changed over the years as the University grew and changed. Degrees were granted from the year 1878. In 1885 there was a name change to the University of Illinois. The school developed the third-largest United States academic library and a creative arts program to match its always-noteworthy scientific area.

University Hall survived until the early 1940's when the ceiling collapsed and the building was condemned and razed because funds needed to repair and maintain it could not be justified.

FIRST BUILDING U. of I.
Champaign-Urbana

ROSCOE
MISSELHORN

OLD STONE FACE—Shawnee National Forest—Harrisburg

This unusual natural rock formation (with its striking resemblance to a human face gazing out from its perch high on a bluff) is in the Saline County Conservation Area, south of the Old Slave House, southeast of Harrisburg, and north of the Garden of the Gods.

Another of the incredible works nature has wrought throughout these Shawnee Hills, it is a part of the similarly-unusual that is found throughout the Shawnee National Forest and the rest of Southern Illinois. The Forest is nearly 250,000 acres of the 800,000 that were designated for possible forest use in October 1933. It is a great band across the state from the Ohio to the Mississippi, narrower in the middle and widening along each river, filled with (and bordered by) a profusion of recreational, scenic, historic and prehistoric sites.

A flyway and wintering area for migrating fowl and other wildlife, it has facilities for practically every sportsman: camping, hunting, fishing, boating, swimming, golfing, horseback riding and hiking. The Ozark-Shawnee Trail alone is some 115 miles, from Grand Tower on the Mississippi to Battery Rock on the Ohio, along the flowing ridges of the Shawnee Hills. It is supplemented by innumerable shorter trails throughout the Forest; the Stone Face Trail itself is about nine miles long and is well-maintained.

The scenic is all about. The historic ranges from Cave-in-Rock and Shawneetown on the Ohio to the Illinois Iron Furnace, the first charcoal-fired iron furnace in Illinois, It operated from 1837 through the Civil War and it supplied the Mound City Naval Yards. It continued to operate during the 1880's and has now been reconstructed. The historic also includes the Trail of Tears State Park near Jonesboro, where the Cherokee wintered before having to cross the Mississippi on their forced move West. It also includes Grand Tower and its Tower Rock National Site in the Mississippi.

Prehistoric sites overlap some of the historic ones, but especially include the ten or so "Stone Forts" or "Walls" (one in Giant City State Park in Southern Illinois, where stacked-stone walls enclose several acres atop an 80-foot sandstone cliff). Also to be found are others: Stonefort—Millstone Bluff (with remains of an Indian village, burial ground, and rock ledge carvings)—Draper's Bluff—Indian Kitchen—War Bluff and others. Some are better-preserved than others, but all are still the subject of conjecture concerning their purpose, and a number of them come fully equipped with legends.

If there are any local legends regarding (Old) Stone Face, they have not yet been recorded nor the formation immortalized as was its eastern cousin by Nathaniel Hawthorne. The Stone Face in the Shawnee Hills still holds its tongue.

STONE FACE
SHAWNEE HILLS

ROSCOE
MISSELHORN

INDEX